MOTIVATING CHILDREN

Behavior Modification in the Classroom

WALTER M. VERNON
Illinois State University
Normal, Illinois

HOLT, RINEHART AND WINSTON, INC.
New York   Chicago   San Francisco   Atlanta
Dallas   Montreal   Toronto   London   Sydney

370.15
V598m

Copyright © 1972 by Holt, Rinehart and Winston, Inc.
All Rights Reserved
Library of Congress Catalog Card Number: 70–184111
ISBN: 0–03–085945–X
Printed in the United States of America
456   090   987654

PREFACE

This is a book for beginners—persons experienced perhaps in teaching, but beginners nevertheless in the principles of operant conditioning. Since this book was not designed as a classroom text, the style of writing was deliberately made simple and communicative, and extensive references to the background research were omitted. Readers with some background in psychology will recognize the ideas of B. F. Skinner in most of the operant concepts. Certain sections of the text are based on the publications of other men such as Wolpe, Bandura, and Ayllon. More sophisticated readers in the subject may discover that, in condensing the carefully developed principles of these men to less formal explanations, I unavoidably sacrificed some specifics. To these readers I must stress again the audience for whom I have written. A great number of the cited experiments, only a portion of which have been published, were conducted on the campuses of Illinois State University and Illinois Wesleyan University. In the event that readers might need citations to specific research, I will respond to their communications.

I feel certain that my own enthusiasm, which surely shows throughout this book, is widely shared. Most psychologists whom I know who were originally trained in traditional clinical approaches to motivation and who have had the opportunity to work closely with those doing operant conditioning have themselves become enthusiastic adherents to the operant approach. I am quite convinced that the general approach described in this book, together with future developments in such areas as perception and biochemistry, will provide the major thrust of psychology in the decades immediately ahead.

As in any endeavor of this sort, a writer must have the benefit of the proper setting and encouragement from the right people. Our education program at Illinois State University is one of the nation's largest and afforded many opportunities that made this task easier. Encouragement from several colleagues on our faculty is appreciated. In particular, I appreciate the encouragement of Dr. William J. Gnagey, the finest teacher I have ever seen operate in a classroom. My father Dodd Vernon, a professional journalist, expended a vast amount of effort in putting many sections of this book into revised form, and my wife Jill did likewise in her attention to clerical details. To them, and to our baby boy Dodd, this book is dedicated. I hope our boy's teachers in future years employ behavior-modification concepts.

Walter M. Vernon

Normal, Illinois
December 1971

CONTENTS

INTRODUCTION 1

The past decade has seen fantastic advances made in the various ways by which man has brought the powerful methods of science to bear upon his problems. Psychology is no exception. A new educational technology called behavior modification has gradually been put together on the basis of laboratory findings, tested, and subjected to further refinements. At a number of centers in the nation, spectacular successes are being achieved through the use of behavior modification methods with normal children as well as with maladjusted and retarded youngsters. It is not unusual to hear of classrooms of children who progress through two or more academic years of material in a single nine-month session.

The field of behavior modification is young. Most experts are concentrating their efforts on research rather than on wide-scale application, and the new methods have not yet found their way into the mainstream of public education. The new technology is visible as yet only in communities near certain large universities, where public school and laboratory school classrooms are involved in research. Many teachers who have seen the effectiveness of the methods tell colleagues or school administrators, but there are so few qualified individuals who can train teachers and set up new programs of behavior modification that administrators are understandably reluctant to initiate changes.

An unfortunate recent development is that many teachers go ahead and, on the basis of certain vague understandings, make mistakes and fail to reach the expected goals, and then abandon their efforts. Perhaps even worse, administrators seek out available school psychologists for advice on behavior-modification programs, not realizing that many of them know little or nothing about behavior modification. Recently a new recipient of a graduate degree in school psychology—one who had systematically avoided taking courses in experimental analysis of behavior or behavior modification—informed me that he had been hired specifically to set up a behavior-modification program for retarded children.

It was for such reasons that this publication was undertaken. There is a growing need for basic information on the new techniques, styled so that applications of principles can be readily undertaken. Careful study of the material presented in this book should enable many classroom teachers to develop additional methods of motivating their classes so as to benefit from the technology of behavior modification.

Background

For years psychologists developed an "educational psychology" that was mainly descriptive, that is, they described patterns of behavior in detail and developed behavioral labels such as *socially inhibited, underachiever, hyperactive,* and the like. The labels, unfortunately, were typically used as if they were the actual causes of behavior. Thus a child was said to have frequent conflicts with others "because he is aggressive," or to be quiet and isolated "because he is socially inhibited." By acting as if *descriptions* of behavior were causes, psychologists became subject to a sort of fatalism. Behavior patterns seemed to be taken for granted, and attempts were made to "understand" behavior in what was essentially an empathic way. The emphasis in psychology was not, until recently, on the direct control of behavior.

Behavior-Oriented Psychologists

The field of psychology contains a number of persons called behavior theorists, who have been conducting research for several decades. *Behavior theory* emphasizes the development of a comprehensive set of interrelated concepts regarding behavior, based upon the relationships between biological drives and the phenomenon known as conditioning. *Conditioning,* in turn, is defined as the simplest form of learning—the simple association, through experience, of events that occur close together in time. Until recently, almost all behavior theorists studied conditioning as a laboratory phenomenon and were not prone to extend their research into areas of practical application. In the last few years, however, two groups of enthusiastic psychologists have emerged from the ranks of behavior theorists, both eager to apply conditioning principles to practical problems of human motivation and personality. Using clinics and classrooms as their work settings, they developed the techniques of behavior modification. The first group, *operant* psychologists (earlier called reinforcement theorists), studies operant conditioning, which concerns only visible behaviors. *Two-factor* theorists are concerned with both operant conditioning and classical conditioning, the latter being essentially the learning of emotional patterns not readily evident from visible behavior. Both operant and two-factor psychologists have produced the subject-matter area we call behavior modification.

Assumptions

Some basic conclusions have been drawn from conditioning research and have served to guide behavior theorists. The following statement of some of these conclusions, or assumptions, gives an indication of the general approach of behavior modification:

1. All behaviors have causes—nothing "just happens."*
2. All behavior changes are "normal"; what looks like "*ab*normal behavior" is only the normal outcome of a person's being in an abnormal environment.
3. Behavior change is primarily the result of systematic changes in the *consequences* of the individual's behavior—this is operant conditioning.
4. Emotional patterns relating to some object or experience, including intense emotions as well as general attitudes and moderate likes and dislikes, are the results of repeated associations of the object in question with other events—this is classical conditioning.
5. One's biological heritage interacts with one's history of conditioning to produce the majority of an individual's behavior patterns.
6. Rational thinking—the kind only human beings are capable of to any significant degree—has much *less* effect than does operant or classical conditioning in determining behavior and emotions.

It is on the basis of these assumptions that we proceed to the subject matter of the most powerful body of principles ever developed for the systematic control of behavior—behavior theory, developed through the experimental method.

* This is the notion of "scientific determinism."

THE THREE LEVELS OF PSYCHOLOGICAL EXPERIENCE

2

Psychological experience exists at three levels: Level 1, *respondent behavior*; Level 2, *operant behavior*; and Level 3, *rational behavior*.

Respondent Behavior

Respondents are reflexive emotional patterns that are elicited by specific stimuli, such as those producing pain. These powerful reflex patterns are unlearned, basically biological responses. Respondents can be categorized into one of three emotional *orientations*. Such stimuli as food and water, contact comfort (contact with soft, warm surfaces), and interesting environmental variety, all of which provide pleasure, bring about an emotional *approach* orientation. Aversive stimulation such as pain, physical irritation, extremes of noise or light, frustration, or physical restraint usually produces an emotional *avoidance* orientation. In those cases in which an aversive stimulus continues and is unavoidable or inescapable, an emotional *aggressive* orientation develops. The characteristic directions of respondent patterns to specific stimuli are generally uniform among the various animal species and human beings. The most important thing to remember at this point is that the term *respondent* refers to how a person *feels* about various circumstances and things in his environment—the physical acting-out of the orientation may be restrained for a number of reasons.

While the *un*learned respondent patterns or reflexes, such as we have described, do not frequently appear to have direct relevance to classroom experiences, respondent patterns that are learned through classical conditioning and are based directly on unlearned respondent patterns, are vital, as we shall see in Chapter 3.

Operant Behavior

While respondents are reflexive reactions, operant behavior is voluntary, in the manner of a person cutting his lawn, reading a newspaper, or playing golf during a relaxed weekend. Operants are generally visible behaviors rather than internal emotions. The name comes from the fact that an operant behavior *operates* on the environment, while a respondent behavior is a response to the environment that does not change it. This is not to say that operants do not often depend upon aspects of the environment for their occurrence. As simple illustrations, one does not go swimming without a lake or pool, students do not begin to ask questions in class until the teacher enters the room, and one does not mow his lawn until such an action is suggested by the height of the grass. Still, these behaviors are clearly voluntary and are not reflexes to the various aspects of the environment.

In summary, while the term *respondent* refers to how a person *feels,* the *operant* is what a person *does*.[1] Laboratory-oriented operant psychologists usually hesitate to refer to unobservables, but we will go so far as to include a person's thought processes as a subcategory of what he does. Thus, when we develop the principles governing operant behavior in a later section, we will at that time consider the sorts of things that affect one's thinking.

Rational Behavior

Most behavior theorists have concerned themselves very little with logical reasoning, anticipation, abstract thinking, and decision making—activities, limited almost exclusively to human beings, that we call the rational processes. Nevertheless, such processes do influence people's subsequent actions. The problem is that many psychologists have given rational thinking, as the prime cause of behavior, a more elevated position than it deserves. Rational thinking, which typically involves reflective reminiscence or the projection of one's thoughts into the future, is usually involved in *how* a person does something, but most of the time such rational processes do not actually determine *what* the person does. What we are saying here is that a child must rationally understand mathematical operations if he is to do math problems, but whether he works on math problems or watches television, whether he does optional extra credit work,

---

[1] The exception being the physical action counterparts of respondent emotions, such as physical approach, physical avoidance, and aggressive behavior. Such actions, when reflexively produced by stimuli, are usually treated as respondent behaviors.

and the like are activities that are under the control of other determinants. Similarly, knowing how to read and why one should read are different matters from actually wanting to read and liking to read.

The Limitations of the Rational Influence

Let us assume that a child "knows" why he should be nice to his little sister. He may be able to state aloud that sister is little and only bad children bully those who are smaller; sister is sweet and does no harm to her brother; and mean people don't go to heaven. Meanwhile, sister continues to be bullied by her brother.

Similarly, a school counselor may see a discouraged high school student who has announced his plans to drop out of school in order to accept a fairly well-paying job. Since the student's motives are economic, he is shown how staying in school will enable him to have better jobs, higher pay, and greater employment security throughout his lifetime. Despite "insight" into these relevant economic factors, the best prediction for a student in such circumstances is that he will go ahead with his plan to drop out.

We all do things that we know we should not do. And, more commonly, we do *not* do things that we know we should. What, then, is the contribution of rational thought and understanding to the ways in which most of us conduct our daily lives? Bertrand Russell, the eminent British philosopher, wrote, ". . . it has been said that man is a rational animal. All of my life I have been searching for evidence which could support this." Although Russell was not a particularly whimsical individual, it is likely that his remark was overstated for greater impact. He may have had in mind the various ways in which man so frequently departs from a rational path.

First, let us realize that there is a very good reason why many people view man as being primarily rational: In many of our daily affairs our conditioned habit patterns complement rather than conflict with the directions of our rational judgments. The student who realizes that education is extremely important is very likely to have had various classroom experiences that were highly rewarding to him. He probably has parents who were supportive in their attitudes toward education. The student's continuance in education is, then, the product of complementary factors. Similarly, an individual may "believe" in the inferiority of persons of some other race. It is practically assured that his rational judgments are complemented by a variety of interactions with his family and peers that have encouraged such feelings.

When people see so many occasions on which their own behaviors or those of others appear to be consistent with rational thinking, it is no wonder that they tend to believe that rationality is the sole factor—or at least the predominant one—in determining behavior patterns. It is necessary, however, that they give fair consideration to the many, many times that man's behavior is contradictory and seems at least a bit irrational. Only in this way can they gain a fair view of the interaction of the determinants of behavior.

At the present time research findings in psychology suggest that where conflict exists between rational tendencies and conditioned habit patterns, either respondent or operant ones, rationality seldom predominates. This is, of course, assuming that conditioned patterns have developed to a meaningful degree. The recognition of this predomination of conditioned patterns is one of the major distinctions between behavior theory and most of the other forms of academic psychology. Many persons, of course, have only a very few opposing tendencies in their own behaviors. There seems good reason to believe that such a lack of conflict is essentially what "mental health" is all about. The sorts of environmental conditions that would foster strong opposing tendencies are generally viewed as being pathological by mental health specialists. Parents who belittle schooling after the child has been stimulated in the classroom by an effective teacher, the child who is in perpetual fear for his personal safety from bigger, older children with whom he must associate daily, the parent who acts affectionately so as to lure the wary child close enough to be seized and punished, and the worried, overwrought parent who gives praise for accomplishments but criticizes the efforts of offspring if they are not perfect are all examples of ways in which opposing tendencies may develop. In such settings children grow up to know the truth about things "rationally," but their conditioning histories may dictate emotions and behaviors that are quite irrational.

We probably all know a number of persons who seem reasonably free from opposing tendencies such as we have just described. They seem not to have emotional "hang-ups" or "mental blocks." In their visible behaviors they may seem totally rational. Now, however, we should ask these questions about a friend whose behavior is under consideration. Is she (or he) secure in her sexual relationships? Could she have gone much further professionally had she not had a tendency to avoid hard work, to avoid authority roles or responsibilities, or to avoid cooperative teamwork relationships? Does she have unhappy episodes or anxieties about the future, which are known to only her closest relations? Does she fail to work effectively with certain types of persons—men, teen-agers, dominant people, and the like? Is she easily frustrated or angered? Most of these tendencies, where they exist, reflect conditioned patterns that work in opposition to what their hosts know, rationally, should be preferred behaviors.

Even some aspects of behavior that at first seem desirable may be the results of conditioned tendencies that outweigh rational values. There are some persons who are so strongly work-oriented that they feel guilty when they are not producing something. In the same vein, some people are so compulsive that even the smallest task will eventually turn into a major effort of revision and reorganization toward eventual perfection. A dominant personality may propel a man up the ladder of industrial management and then ruin his family relations. Finally, who doesn't know the generally effective teacher who "teaches" all the time—even over the coffee cup with his colleagues? All these people may rationally realize that they are suffering in one sense or another but cannot control themselves.

We hope that the reader has now gained insight into what we mean by saying that conditioned tendencies are prone to dominate rational ones. Unfortunately, many persons feel they can help cure most of the problems of others simply by helping the person with the problem reach an understanding of why he behaves the way he does. In the further reading of this book, it may become clear that there are a number of alternative approaches, most of which have been shown to be highly effective in the remediation of human problems.

CLASSICAL CONDITIONING

3

The Learning of Respondent Patterns

Remember that we have described respondent development through learning as the factor that determines a person's general feelings about certain people, places, or things. Obviously this is an area that is important to the classroom teacher, both so that she may understand the children in her classroom, and so that she may most effectively enter into the process of the student's emotional development.

Unlearned respondent patterns—reflexes as they are often termed—are natural sorts of reactions to a variety of stimuli. It is important at this point to differentiate clearly among the three emotional orientations and the sorts of situations that produce them. Following is a diagram that may be of help:

Type of Stimulus	Emotional Orientation	Typical Mental Experience
Pleasant and rewarding	Approach	Like
Unpleasant, but escapable	Avoidance	Dislike, possibly fear
Unpleasant and inescapable	Aggression	Hate, possibly fear

On the day of his birth, the child responds positively or negatively to a variety of things in his immediate environment. Moreover, other respondent patterns emerge as the child matures that, although correlated with development, are still reflexive and unlearned. The table on page 10 traces some of the unconditioned response linkages.

Although we are most directly interested in the various sorts of *learned* or conditioned respondent patterns, the unconditioned stimulus / response linkage is of critical importance. This is because learned patterns can only

9

develop in the presence of the stimuli that elicit the reflexive emotional responses. Thus, the primitive, biological reactions inherent in the un-learned respondent pattern form the necessary base for the developmental event that we will hereafter refer to as *classical conditioning*.

AN INVENTORY OF A FEW OF THE UNLEARNED RESPONDENT PATTERNS

Stimulus	Emotional Orientation
Food	Approach
Water	Approach
Sexual access (mature organisms)	Approach
Environmental change, variety	Approach
Contact comfort (cuddling)	Approach
Pain, or other physical distress	Avoidance
Environmental "sameness"	Avoidance
Inescapable punishment	Aggression
Prolonged blocking of goal-directed activity	Aggression
Failure of reward to be delivered after arrival at goal	Aggression

From the first day of birth, the infant begins to acquire classically conditioned respondent patterns. While his physical drives are being satisfied, the pleasures of nursing, being cuddled, and so forth are associated with people's attention. In this way people's attention becomes a pleasant event in itself. In a similar manner, being picked up is a situational stimulus that repeatedly accompanies being fed and other sorts of pleasant events, so that the child begins to respond positively to being lifted up.

Stated abstractly, we would say that classical conditioning occurs when a stimulus that already produces a respondent emotional pattern is repeatedly paired with a neutral stimulus such as a person, thing, or general situation. After a number of such pairings, the initially neutral stimulus begins to take on emotion-producing characteristics. It is simpler to refer to the stimuli by standard names. The stimulus that "naturally" produces a respondent pattern is called an *unconditioned stimulus*, or UCS, and the emotion produced by the UCS is called the unconditioned response. Unconditioned simply means there is no need for conditioning in order for a response to occur—for example, the first time an infant experiences pain, he reacts emotionally. The UCS is paired with a neutral stimulus, called the *conditioned stimulus* or CS. When the CS alone is finally able to produce the respondent pattern, the pattern is called a conditioned response. The conditioning process, for example, whereby a person shows a general fear of dogs after being painfully bitten, may be diagrammed in this manner:

```
UCS ─────────────────➤ R
     pain        ⟋↗        fear
              ⟋
           ⟋
        ⟋
     CS⟋
      dog
```

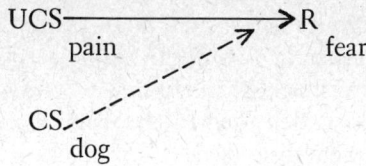

Notice that both the unconditioned response and the conditioned response are of the same basic pattern. The painful attack produced fear; subsequently the approach of a dog produces fear. In certain cases, where the UCS is extremely strong, the CS can produce the emotion after a single conditioning experience.

Examples of Classical Conditioning

The following actual experiment is a simple one, intended to illustrate how a neutral stimulus can acquire emotion-producing properties. Each of a group of male college students had an electric shock-delivery apparatus attached to two of his fingers. When a two-second shock of low intensity was delivered, the heart rates showed a marked elevation. (The heart rate is a measurable physical element of the emotion elicited by shock.) Each time shock was delivered, a soft buzzer was sounded simultaneously. Several minutes were allowed between sessions for the heart rate to return to normal. After twenty pairings of the two stimuli, the buzzer was sounded by itself. Immediately, there was a heart rate increase. The diagram that illustrates this conditioning procedure is the following:

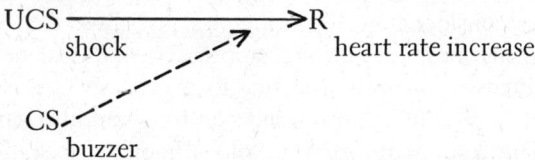

```
UCS ─────────────────➤ R
     shock       ⟋↗        heart rate increase
              ⟋
           ⟋
        ⟋
     CS⟋
      buzzer
```

Lest we think that rational processes were at work and that the buzzer simply provided a rationally understood message that a shock was due, consider what happened next. The shock-delivery apparatus was disconnected and put away; the subjects had the opportunity of seeing this occur and were than asked to try *not* to react to the buzzer; then the buzzer sounded again. The result was the same—another heart rate increase. From such findings we can see that the response to the CS, just like the response to the shock itself, was involuntary and reflexive. It was not influenced in the slightest by a rational understanding of the reality of the situation.

In another case, college students were given an attitude test that measured their feelings toward various national groups. Then, at spaced intervals, a short list of names of nations was sounded several times from a tape recorder. Each time either of two South American countries' names was sounded, a mild electric shock was delivered to one group of the subjects, and an offensive odor was delivered to the other group. After several such pairings, the students were dismissed. A few weeks later the students were reassembled and given the attitude tests again. The results showed sharp increases in prejudice toward people from both of the South American countries named in the conditioning procedure.

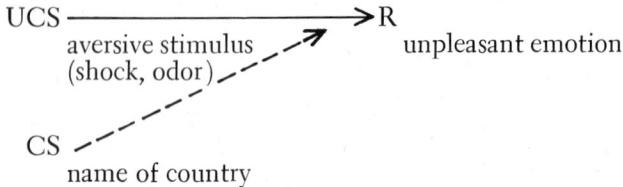

UCS ──────────────────→ R
    aversive stimulus   ⟋   unpleasant emotion
    (shock, odor) ⟋
           ⟋
           ⟋
    CS ⟋
    name of country

The shock group and the odor group both showed this change. No attitude changes occurred toward the other nationalities named in the attitude test. There is no "rational" basis for such changes. It deserves mention again, of course, that in a very large proportion of cases persons *do* respond in a manner consistent with rational awareness and are thus made more prone to interpret their feelings in terms of rational understanding.

Classical Conditioning in Everyday Life

Let us consider how the principles just illustrated apply to general, everyday situations. Conditioned-approach emotional orientations are numerous. Animals and children show "love" for persons associated with pleasant things such as feeding, contact comfort, stimulus variety, and the like. Nostalgia in later years for the "old school" is seen in people who have had many pleasant experiences there. Attachments to houses, automobiles, books already read, certain relatives, favorite social groups, and cities are in almost direct proportion to the relative amounts of rewarding experiences associated with these "CSs."

Conditioned-avoidance emotional orientations are also numerous. Some people do not care for group activities, participant sports, reading material, education, spicy food, church attendance, competition, examinations, specific areas of academic subject matter, or even the opposite sex. The past histories of such persons typically show a greater proportion of unpleasant than pleasant experiences associated with the stimulus in question.

Conditioned-aggressive emotional orientations are very much in evidence in many school-age children. In the cases of certain children—the low-achieving group—abuse from teachers and failure serve as *inescapable* aversive UCSs, eliciting irritation and anger. The CSs that are consistently paired with failure and continued frustration include the school itself and the teachers. Assaults against school property and teachers are common. Those perpetrating the assaults are, with only a few exceptions, the low achievers. Also, the same youngsters who learned to associate authority figures in the school or in the home with inescapable unpleasant experiences become the adults whose emotional orientation toward other authority figures, such as policemen, is aggressive.

Some Principles

We have already illustrated the definitive principle that is the basis for classical conditioning:

1. A neutral stimulus (CS), when paired with a stimulus (UCS) that elicits a respondent emotional orientation, becomes capable of eliciting the same emotional orientation.

Other important basic principles of classical conditioning are:

2. If the UCS is of high intensity, the magnitude of the response to it is strong; weak UCSs produce weak unconditioned responses.
3. If the UCS during conditioning is of high intensity, a response to the CS that is developed through conditioning is relatively strong; weak UCSs in conditioning produce weak conditioned responses.

It might be pointed out that just a few years ago experimenters, using dogs, showed that an animal could be brought to a condition of extreme panic the second time it heard a bell if, on the occasion of the bell's first presentation, the accompanying UCS was a shock of paralyzing intensity and with a duration of several seconds. In much the same way, human beings occasionally suffer an intense trauma and subsequently fear the sort of stimuli that were in the general situation in which the trauma occurred.

4. The more times a UCS is paired with a CS, the stronger the response to the CS becomes, until it approaches the strength of the response to the UCS itself.
5. After a CS becomes capable of eliciting a response, the mere passage of time does *not* weaken the eliciting power of the CS.

In a famous experiment some years ago, the subject, a dog, which had experienced a bell paired with strong electric shock, was sent to live on a farm for nearly four years. At the end of that time he was brought into the laboratory again, where he heard the bell ring. He showed just as strong an emotional reaction as he had shown in response to the bell just before he had been sent away.

6. Response to the CS, once established, does *not* become weaker if the UCS is subsequently presented in the absence of the CS.
7. Response to the CS, once established, *does* become weaker if the CS is subsequently presented in the absence of the UCS.

The last principle refers to a process called *extinction* of classically conditioned responses. Extinction is gradual, and its degree depends upon the number of CS presentations experienced by the individual that are unaccompanied by the UCS.

8. After a CS becomes capable of eliciting a response, stimuli similar to the CS will elicit some degree of that response.

Principle number eight refers to *stimulus generalization*. This is the process by which an aggressive child, made that way by a brutal father, comes to resent all male authority figures—policemen, school officials, and others. Their shared stimulus characteristic of being male authority figures provides the necessary similarity for stimulus generalization to occur. This is also the process underlying the familiar experience of liking or disliking an individual almost immediately upon the first meeting. When this happens, it is because we perceive similarities in that individual to persons who already bring out strong feelings in us.

The principle of stimulus generalization lies behind most of our emotional experiences. Seldom do we encounter the exact same situation that originally was traumatic or pleasurable. If we "like" John Wayne movies, part of our reaction is a generalized response from the previous occasions when we viewed John Wayne movies and were highly entertained. If we think a particular name for a child is pretty, it is often at least partly due to memories of other people who have borne that name. A social psychologist in the 1930s even found that young ladies whose fathers wore moustaches married young men with moustaches significantly more frequently than did young ladies with smooth-shaven fathers. Moreover, a subgroup made up of young ladies whose relationships with their fathers were characterized by strife and a lack of affection showed exactly the opposite pattern of mate selection. Perhaps you may wonder at this point about the real (rational?) nature of "true love."

In a more relevent vein, the phenomenon of stimulus generalization is involved when a student says he prefers male teachers or likes a certain area of academic work. Such characteristics as "cowardice" reflect generalizations from earlier experiences in which the individual was traumatized by certain other individuals. One can hardly overemphasize the pervasiveness of the phenomenon called stimulus generalization. It pops up everywhere, and some of its effects are quite serious.

A Case of Stimulus Generalization

Recently we were consulted by a mother who was worried about an emotional problem of her third-grade daughter, who was an only child. The girl had had a seemingly normal preschool history, except that she had become increasingly shy with strangers from about the third or fourth year of her life. At about the time she entered school, however, she began to act completely like a mute in the presence of adults outside the family. She talked freely with the mother, with the grandmother who lived in the same town, and with her same-aged friends. In school the child was performing reasonably well on exercises and quizzes, and had earned promotion each year to the next grade, despite the fact that, as far as any school personnel could tell, she had never uttered a word to a teacher, either spontaneously or in answer to a direct question. She seemed well-adjusted in her relations with other little girls and boys, and typically chattered happily on the playground, stopping her speech if a teacher approached the group.

These facts, plus some elaboration and examples, proved to be all that the mother could offer as background material for speculation. At that point it seemed that the most probable hypothesis was that the child was showing a conditioned-avoidance emotional orientation, brought on by a harsh teacher in an earlier grade. Why else would the child tense at the prospect of direct interaction with teachers? Another reason to believe that the condition had originated in the school was because the child was apparently spontaneous and relaxed in her interactions with the mother. A careful exploration of the child's school experiences, year by year, however, failed to turn up any "incident" that might have precipitated the extreme emotional pattern that existed. The next step had to be a consideration of all incidents in the home. It did not appear likely that the mother–daughter relationships of the past could have had much to do with the present pattern. It did seem odd, however, that the father had been so seldom referred to in the discussion. Exploration of the father–daughter relationship revealed that the father had been quite impatient with the ordinary demands of a child's care and rearing, and had since become somewhat remote from family interaction. The conversation revealed that at the time of the girl's early acquisition and development of speech, prior to her entering the first grade of school, the father had shown occasional irritation at her halting speech and misuse or mispronunciation of words. The father had occasionally blown up and shouted at the child to hurry up and say what she had to say, and in the cases of mispronunciations he had loudly demanded that she repeat a word over and over until she achieved proper pronunciation.

Why had the little girl responded so drastically to teachers? Only a certain amount of information is available for speculation. In order to explain the generalization of the emotional response from the original father-stimulus to the teachers, we must begin by looking for shared stimulus characteristics. The mother in this case was a very passive, submissive sort of person who confirmed that the father was authoritative and dominant —the one who made the rules and enforced discipline in the family. These characteristics almost exactly match many of the necessary role behaviors of elementary-level teachers. It is also probable that during the first weeks of school the teachers had stated rules, admonitions, and directions, which were "father-type" behaviors to the girl. There may well have been a certain amount of emphasis upon vocabulary development and speaking out loud with correct pronunciation—areas of considerable sensitivity to the little girl.

Many times, emotional generalization will proceed along the stimulus dimensions of sex, race, or age. This case, however, shows how a behavioral stimulus can operate. Female teachers were much more similar to the little girl's father than to her mother.

Treatment in this case began with a number of conversations on the telephone—the girl speaking with various adult relatives and friends of the family. Then the girl spoke to her third-grade teacher, then the teachers of her past experience, by telephone. The conversations were pleasant and, the teachers' visual cues being absent, not particularly anxiety-provoking. With very little additional help, the girl began to interact on her own with her teacher in the classroom, and soon practically all of the problems that had been observed had disappeared. Unfortunately the mother viewed this as a satisfactory conclusion to the case and went no further with remediation. One cannot help but wonder about the child's future interactions with a variety of dominant male figures, both in and out of the classroom situation.

9. After a CS is well established in its capability of eliciting an emotional response, other neutral stimuli, upon being paired with the CS, will acquire some degree of the same emotion-producing characteristics.

Principle number nine is called *higher-order conditioning*. Through classical conditioning such as we have already described, stimuli such as approval and praise acquire positive, rewarding characteristics. Higher-order conditioning would then take place when the praise of another person is associated with the cues accompanying the completion of a project or a lengthy, difficult task. After a while, when one finishes a project, there is a very positive feeling of satisfaction that goes quite beyond relief that further effort is not required. In this manner, given the appropriate environment to foster such development, many people become capable of considerable sustained effort, which is then followed by a sense of satisfaction and pride in their accomplishment. People exhibit many quite complex patterns of higher-order conditioning. Even lower animals, such as dogs, are capable of strong emotional responses developed through higher-order conditioning.

The phenomenon of higher-order conditioning is also valuable in explaining how certain problems can arise. This is how a person can acquire fears and anxieties concerning stimuli that have never been directly associated with any actual physical pain or threat.

Overview

To understand emotional responses to environmental stimuli is an extremely important ability in the classroom teacher. This is not because she should be expert in reducing the level of intense fear or hostility. Serious emotional matters would be best referred to mental health personnel. Rather, the teacher should clearly understand that for the few months of her supervision, the development of the child's emotional structure—a complex and far-reaching fabric of likes, dislikes, aversions, and attachments that may last a lifetime—is largely in her hands. If she is an English teacher whose materials or manner of presenting them creates high levels of aversion, then the end-product is predictable. Although difficult to put into practice, literature assignments should be individualized at least to the extent that every student has material that he can at least understand. The alternative is permanent avoidance of reading. A 1969 Gallup poll established that high school graduates in the over–twenty-one age group had read an average of *less* than one book during the twelve preceding months. Since a few people read many books, this indicates that most high school graduates do not read books at all after their graduation. The book-avoiding student is often the product of the teaching practices to which he has been exposed.

Certain math teachers should accept responsibility for the many students in college who have "mental blocks" with mathematics and who freeze in their seats when topics such as statistics are introduced in some of their courses. Another group of students avoids a foreign language, if allowed by a university's degree requirements. Concerning the last two fields mentioned, nowhere in the junior high or high school curriculum are there so many opportunities as in math and foreign language courses to humiliate students in front of other people. "Going to the blackboard" or "rising to translate" leaves many students with an enormous negative emotional residual.

Any teacher who, for the sake of "high standards" or for any other reason, inflicts misery, boredom, embarrassment, or humiliation on students to the extent that they avoid the subject matter thereafter, fails completely to be an effective teacher. On the other hand, good teaching has its emotional payoffs. Affection for subject matter is often developed in the classrooms.

Illustration

In 1967 I gave a questionnaire to more than three hundred university students, mostly freshmen. The first question asked for the name of their finest high school teacher—the one who could communicate and teach better than all the others. Question two asked for that teacher's subject field. Question three asked for the student's major field of study at the university. The answer to question one was written before the students heard the next questions. In view of the large number of university major fields offered, identical answers to questions two and three, on the basis of chance alone, should have been within the range of 4 percent to 6 percent. The agreement, however, was 41 percent. Considering the number of university major fields that are not even offered as courses in high school, as well as the number of "undeclared major" students, the 41 percent figure was truly remarkable.

Perhaps this gives an insight into the true meaning of good teaching. The good teacher's students continue in later years to study and learn further. The reason is that the subject matter (CS) has been repeatedly associated with pleasant, interesting experiences (UCSs) in the classroom, until the subject matter itself eventually produces pleasure and enjoyment.

OPERANT CONDITIONING

4

The Control of Behavior through Its Consequences

During the early 1960s the first massive research in human operant conditioning began. The basic idea behind operant conditioning is quite simple: *Behavior is controlled by its consequences*. Let us see what that means.

Example

Joe was a five-year-old Negro boy, who acted as if he were afraid of white adults. In the kindergarten class, which he shared with two other black children and twenty-two white children, he was withdrawn and socially isolated. One day he was taken to the university laboratory, where the experimenter met him and made him comfortable. "Joe," said the experimenter, "We're going to play a get-acquainted game. I'll ask you about yourself and you answer. Sometimes, when you answer, I'll give you a surprise. Where do you live, Joe—in this city?" After a moment, Joe nodded his head. "That's good, Joe," said the experimenter as he gave Joe a foil-wrapped piece of chocolate. "But from now on you'll have to talk to me—don't just nod your head. Okay?" "Okay," said Joe. "Fine," said the experimenter, who gave him the second piece. "Now, you eat those two, and then we'll talk some more."

Within fifteen minutes, with this continuing procedure, Joe was a chatterbox. Such behavior with a white adult was a total reversal of a social pattern with which the kindergarten teacher had admitted complete defeat. Behavior was being controlled by its consequences. The consequences of conversing were chocolate rewards. These rewards are called *reinforcers*, and the result of reinforcement is *operant conditioning*.

Reinforcement

Reinforcement is more than just a bribe—something superficial in the behavioral process. It is one of the strongest laws of behavioral science that when an individual's actions are followed by satisfying consequences, those actions tend, thereafter, to increase. For example, if, by complaining, a person gets certain people's attention and sympathy, the person tends to gripe and complain even more frequently thereafter. The corollary of this rule is that when actions do *not* produce satisfactions, the rates of those actions begin to fall off.

As we shall see, candy rewards have occasionally been used. Other consequences, such as gold stars on a chart, the teacher's praise, or simply her attention, are familiar and effective reinforcers. The teacher who is considering the use of reinforcement should be aware of the degree to which the majority of human behavior is controlled by rewards. In practically every activity, adults' as well as children's habitual behavior patterns are those that have produced payoffs in the past. The adult's parents, friends, professional associates, and formal contact groups have provided many of these payoffs.

To consider what a simple reinforcer such as attention can to do influence even a teacher's behavior, we shall consider a little "experiment" that, to our knowledge, has been performed effectively several times, with minor variations. It usually begins with a university class entering into a "conspiracy" to control an aspect of their teacher's behavior. The target behavior is typically something like lecturing from one of the extreme corners of the front of the classroom. As the class period begins, the students all appear to be paying a great deal more attention to the tops of their desks than to the teacher. As the teacher moves about, and is sooner or later near the appropriate corner, the class miraculously begins to pay rapt attention. The attention is lost each time the teacher moves away from the corner. Long before the end of the fifty-minute class period, the teacher is staying in the corner of the room almost continuously—a very irrational behavior. Such a game assumes more serious proportions when we consider the implications, for education, of the ability to control the behaviors of intelligent human beings through such simple means.

Primary Reinforcement

When certain things are *naturally* rewarding, like candy, food, and environmental variety, such rewards are called *primary* reinforcers. The alert reader may notice that these are the same types of stimuli that we referred to earlier as UCSs. A large number of experiments using primary reinforcers have been conducted with children.

Case One

The first illustration involves learning to count and use numbers. Charlie was "borrowed" from a summer Headstart class for an hour a day. This almost-five-year-old was so slow in his progress that his teacher suspected retardation. After several weeks of effort, she said, Charlie still could not count to ten. Begging and pleading had not succeeded. Charlie acted bored and soon looked away from the teacher to see what the other children in the room were doing. It was decided that there should be consequences for correct responding. A wired board with ten small light bulbs in a row was prepared in a workshop. Either the first one, the first two, the first three, and so on, or all of the bulbs could be turned on by the experimenter. The experimenter began with one light, which Charlie correctly called "one." Then came two, then three, and so forth until Charlie had gone to ten, missing three along the way. Each time he was right, Charlie was rewarded with a foil-wrapped piece of chocolate. The procedure then changed from a regular sequence (1-2-3) to a mixed sequence. Also, when the lights were illuminated, it was about thirty seconds before the experimenter asked Charlie for his answer. And, while candy was delivered immediately if the answer was correct, it was thirty more seconds after Charlie's answer before the next lights in the sequence were illuminated. This delay procedure served the purpose of having Charlie empty-handed much of the time, and so made an error costly in terms of having no candy to eat for minute-long intervals. Whenever Charlie made a mistake, instead of being given candy, he was told the answer that he should have given. Within eighteen minutes Charlie was master of the 1 through 10 sequence, not only in sequential counting but also in recognizing individual groups and giving the proper number. Another few minutes established Charlie as master of 11 through 20 as well, this being done on the spur of the moment using squares of paper lined up on the floor. Charlies had never had much reason for paying attention in order to learn numbers. A handful of bite-size bits of chocolate, however, provided all the reason he needed.

Case Two

That children learn proper social behavior, as well as academic material, is of concern to most teachers. In a laboratory experiment twenty eight-year-old "maladjusted" children were divided into ten teams. On different days, each team was shown how to perform a team task to receive jelly bean reinforcers. The task was to turn two spring-tension pointers to the number 5 on two nine-position dials installed several feet apart. This could not be done by one child alone. The two children on a team had to act simultaneously in order to trigger a dispenser positioned between the dials that released one jelly bean. After instruction, the teams began and all managed to gain three or four jelly beans before difficulties developed. As might be expected, the more socially aggressive child always took the candy until the other member refused to continue. The children were left in the situation, however, and soon the experimenters observed a good deal of maneuvering and "treaty making." Within twenty minutes all of the teams were working productively, with the children cooperating in the task and sharing the proceeds of their efforts fairly. After several days of involvement in this situation, the experimenters observed a spread of the cooperation effect to a number of other activities. The children involved in this experiment had shown little if any evidence of cooperative behavior prior to the experiment. Social behavior in this maladjusted class had been a focus of the teacher's efforts for weeks before the experimental treatment, but her tactics had been traditional—imploring the children to cooperate, pointing out the logical advantages and ethical reasons for cooperation and sharing, and using punishment. These approaches failed. The development of cooperation and sharing in every one of these emotionally disturbed children was made simple, however, through reinforcement of cooperation and nonreinforcement of selfish behavior.

A Case of Primary Reinforcement with Infants

A little more than a decade ago a well-known American psychologist established that infant monkeys have an inborn need for a soft, warm surface to cuddle against. Even if it is provided only by a large, terrycloth-covered doll, the infant monkey with opportunities for such cuddling shows considerably better adjustment than a monkey with no such opportunities. Human infants appear to have similar needs. If left unattended in cribs except for diaper changes, with their bottles suspended upside down from clamps over the cribs, infants cry a great deal, grow listless, and gain little weight, and there is evidence of a very high mortality rate in records of institutions where such techniques were once commonly used. One can say that the need for *contact comfort*, like the need for food, is a primary (unlearned) need, and contact comfort can serve the purpose of being a primary reinforcer to an infant.

A few years ago, twenty couples living in a university housing development, each of whom had a child less than one year old, were selected from volunteers for an experiment. All the mothers selected had stated that their babies were fed on schedule, and that the child's crying ordinarily did not bring about a more immediate feeding. They did, however, usually pick up their babies and provide contact comfort when they cried. The instructions to the mothers for the first phase of the experiment were that they maintain a chart or record of how many times their baby cried and that the parent should continue doing whatever he or she was in the habit of doing at such times. At the end of two weeks the charts were collected, and the mothers were then given basic information about how reinforcement operates and were issued new instructions. The charting of crying was to continue, but now the parents were to try to refrain from picking up the child while he cried, or even immediately thereafter. Nor were they to pick up the child when he was emotionally neutral, unless it was actually necessary. The parents were to try to anticipate his needs for food or changes of physical position and take care of these needs before crying began. They were asked to watch for his good moods and to pick him up frequently and cuddle him when he was laughing or smiling. Hopefully they could do this so frequently that the child would still be picked up as often as before. This part of the program lasted for four weeks. The twenty mothers then met, with their charts, to discuss the results.

According to the charts, crying had been significantly reduced in all twenty babies. The average number of crying incidents per day during the four-week second phase was less than one-half of the number observed during phase one. Also, the mothers generally agreed that their babies appeared to be happier and laughed a great deal more than before. It was the experimenter's impression that all twenty mothers would continue on their own with this technique.

The analysis of the example just presented is quite simple. Prior to the experimental treatment, crying had been reinforced each time the child was picked up. The experimental treatment simply called for the reverse procedure of reinforcing pleasant behavior, so that it increased, while reinforcement of crying ceased.

Overview of Primary Reinforcement

Primary reinforcers are the stimuli that satisfy the primary drives, which are a collection of biological motives. Most teachers will seldom use primary reinforcement. Exceptions may take place where teachers work with very young, mentally retarded, autistic, or grossly maladjusted children, as well as in some special cases that will be described in the next section. The operation of primary reinforcement has been described largely to introduce a discussion of *conditioned* reinforcers, which are much more frequently employed in classrooms.

Conditioned Reinforcement

A great many "rewards" in life are things that we *learn* to appreciate. The list of conditioned reinforcers is much longer than the list of primary ones. Also, in conditioned reinforcement we see a great deal of individual variation in *what* is reinforcing to *whom*.

Money is a simple conditioned reinforcer to use as an illustration. When a coin is given to a baby, he looks at it, feels and tastes it, and then quickly loses interest. The coin only begins to assume importance and subsequently takes on reinforcing characteristics after it is associated with primary reinforcers, as when a young child is given a coin and is told to push it across the counter to a clerk in exchange for an ice cream bar or candy.

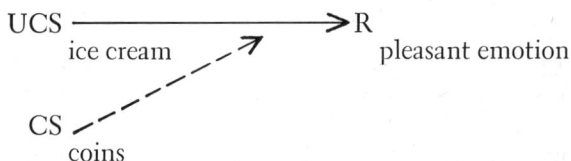

$$
\begin{array}{l}
\text{UCS} \longrightarrow \text{R} \\
\quad \text{ice cream} \nearrow \qquad\qquad \text{pleasant emotion} \\
\quad\quad \nearrow \\
\text{CS} \nearrow \\
\quad \text{coins}
\end{array}
$$

In this manner coins acquire the ability to elicit a pleasant emotion. As you can see, *conditioned reinforcers are developed through being* CSs in a classical conditioning model.

The Four Social Reinforcers

Some conditioned reinforcers are called *social reinforcers* because, instead of being tangible, they are actually social interchanges. Four social reinforcers are generally recognized, all of them developed through classical conditioning.

The first social reinforcer is *attention*. Attention is presumed to be initially neutral. From the first day of a baby's life, the satisfaction of practically every need is paired with someone's attention. Reductions of hunger, thirst, and temperature extremes, as well as reductions of the cumulative needs for environmental variety and contact comfort, are all accompanied by attention. In a short time attention itself comes to elicit a pleasant emotion and at this point can function as a social reinforcer.

Affection is the second social reinforcer. Affection is paired with contact comfort (cuddling), feeding, and various sorts of environmental variety, such as the bath and presentation of new toys. Such activities are frequently occasions for a great deal of vocal and physical display of maternal affection.

The third social reinforcer is *approval*. Approval is, to a great extent, verbal in its administration. Therefore, approval awaits an appreciable degree of language fluency for its development as a reinforcer. The first primary reinforcers to be associated with approval are usually sugar-based foods and contact comfort. When children get a little older, approval also is paired with various stimuli that already have developed as conditioned reinforcers. This, as was previously discussed, results in continued strengthening of approval as a motive through the process called higher-order conditioning. In this way money, the attention of others, and the granting of privileges may all be associated with, and further strengthen, approval as a social reinforcer.

The *submission of others* is the fourth social reinforcer and usually is the last to begin its visible development. Parents are often involved in the development of this reinforcer when their capitulation to the child's tactics is also the occasion for the acquisition of other reinforcers. Suppose that a child wants some of his mother's fresh cookies shortly before mealtime. After first saying no, the mother, faced with the child's continued demands, finally gives in. The submission of another person has been paired with a primary reinforcer. After a number of such pairings, the submission of others itself becomes a reinforcer, and the child begins to enjoy "bossing" and having others obey his orders. In addition, the mother's act reinforces whatever specific behavior finally acquires the cookies, and her child subsequently is even more of a whiner, crier, demander, or tantrum-thrower.

The reinforcing properties of submission by others continues its development when older or stronger children acquire toys or treats by taking them away from other children. It is probably for this reason that a recent study of adults who had been reared in two-child families showed first-borns, on the average, to be considerably more dominant in peer relations than second-borns.

Levels of Reinforcers

It is often useful to conceive of a hierarchy of reinforcers, ranging from primary reinforcement to those conditioned reinforcers that are usually developed through higher-order conditioning. Food, money, praise, and knowledge represent ascending levels of reinforcers. The child is affected last, if at all, by the situational stimuli that make up the highest, most subtle levels.

In the classroom, it is tempting to seek the highest level of reinforcer that a pupil will respond to and then simply use that reinforcer as ingeniously as possible to achieve the goals of the moment. The *development* of higher levels of reinforcers, however, is of more ultimate value to the student. Most retarded and maladjusted youngsters, and occasionally individuals in "normal" classrooms, respond at only the lowest levels of the reinforcer hierarchy. In special education classrooms, if food or money (or tokens; see Chapter 8) is to be used, such reinforcement should be constantly paired with praise. It is not too difficult, through the use of this technique, to develop responsiveness to praise. Soon the teacher can mix food-plus-praise reinforcers with a few instances of praise alone, followed by a gradual increase in the proportion of praise, without any lessening of the reinforcement effect.

A few individuals are fortunate enough to experience the proper circumstances in their homes or schools for the development of *discovery* or *knowing* as a conditioned reinforcer. The development occurs as the student's insights are paired with reinforcement. The student may mention his insight or mastery of some concept, or the teacher may make a verbal reference to the nature of the knowledge just attained by the student. The teacher should immediately interact with the student—perhaps relating the new ability to practical uses—and give approval and praise. The final product of such procedures is a student who appears to be "self-reinforcing," in that he enjoys studying and learning. Such a student is said to be *intrinsically* motivated, but it would appear that intrinsic motivation exists only where extrinsic satisfactions (reinforcers) have been attained previously. Most children are not reared in settings where serious, long-range attempts are made to encourage a love of academics. Even where the attempts are made, they generally fail because of reliance on techniques that do not work. Only a few persons, as adults, are excited by learning and discovery; those few persons sometimes devote their entire lives to academic study and research. You might consider, for a moment, the typical teacher's approach to discovery through the use of the dictionary or an encyclopedia. When the child is assigned something to look up and copy, it is very seldom that any reinforcer accompanies his completion of the project. Rather, the motivation was in terms of what would happen to him if he did not do the assignment, and the only consequence of the completion is usually a relief to be through with the drudgery of the effort. Each classroom teacher should continually try to make new knowledge develop under conditions in which the acquisition of the knowledge leads to on-the-spot reinforcement. Later, when children are given encyclopedia sets, they may then seem to experience pleasure with the contents and spend many hours in self-sustained study.

The conception of intrinsic motivation just described is radically different from the more traditional ways of looking at the matter. The common tendency is to blame failure to be attracted to academic endeavors on either an intellectual limitation of the child or a lack of desire for which the child is typically held to blame. The teacher's role, however, as well as the parents', is the critical factor. The development of academically oriented students by the systematic use of the principles of classical and operant conditioning is within the reach of all classroom teachers.

The Importance of Operant Reinforcement in Education

We have described how patterns of behavior develop through primary as well as conditioned reinforcement. We have shown that conditioned reinforcers may be either tangible items or (more often) social reinforcers, and that neutral stimuli can be systematically developed as reinforcers where they do not already have that characteristic.

At this point we shall advance the view that operant reinforcement principles *predominate* in the behavioral development of human beings. A person's characteristic social habits and work patterns are those that have gained him the most consistent or greatest reinforcement. His less frequently used behavior patterns are arranged in a sort of hierarchy, according to their relative effectiveness in procuring reinforcers. Most of these patterns are stubbornly resistant to an individual's conscious efforts to change himself. While there are underlying temperament differences in people that account for a degree of the variation in their energy and activity levels, aggression, responsiveness, nervousness, and the like, the majority of differences among the behavior patterns of individual human beings are attributable to differences in their conditioning histories.

A vital point that gives further reason to emphasize the use of rewards in education is that every instance of *operant* conditioning involves *simultaneous classical conditioning*. When a teacher reinforces a child's performance, all the possible CSs in the situation—teacher, subject matter, and school—are being paired with the UCS properties of the reinforcer. This, essentially, is how attitudes toward education are acquired by children.

We have discussed the technology of operant reinforcement almost as if the principles were unknown until recently. This is true only in a formal sense. Whenever pronounced behavior change has been produced as the result of one person's influence upon others, the principles of reinforcement have been placed into operation. Many outstanding teachers, through the natural operations of their own personalities, have served as excellent agents of reinforcement in the classroom. Their pleasantness toward all children, patience with the slow, joy in the swift, and faith in the deviant prove effective without any formal training in operant principles. Relatively few such "natural" teachers exist, however. Most teachers can be aided by the knowledge of the formal principles of reinforcement. And, from our own observations, we know that many teachers who have maintained discipline and forced progress only through the use of punitive measures have been assisted to a reversal of their methods and have become much more effective in the process.

In the following sections, various illustrations of operant reinforcement will be given, as well as some finer points of technology. For the moment, however, let us briefly summarize what has been said in this section:

1. Operant conditioning refers to the control of behavior by its consequences.

2. A reward, or satisfying consequence to a behavior, is called a reinforcer; reinforcers tend to increase the rates of the behaviors that produce them.

3. Primary reinforcers are the objects or conditions that reduce the so-called primary drives—hunger, thirst, need for variety in one's environment, and so forth.

4. Conditioned reinforcers are objects or circumstances that have come to be rewarding or satisfying; such objects or circumstances acquire their reinforcing properties through being associated (in classical conditioning) with stimuli that are already reinforcing.

5. In a carefully constructed environment, it is possible for the teacher to develop various social stimuli into conditioned reinforcers, even though the reinforcing characteristic is initially lacking.

6. If the development described above is carried far enough, and done carefully, it is possible to develop self-reinforcing capacities in the child; this is what is involved, essentially, in the expressions "intrinsic motivation" and "love of learning."

7. Every instance of operant conditioning involves simultaneous classical conditioning. If we reward behavior, then in addition to increasing its rate, we develop enjoyment of the general situation in which the rewards occurred; punishment, obviously, has the reverse effect.

8. Finally, we made the point that there are certain teachers who employ proper operant procedures as a natural inclination, but most of us can profit from an awareness of the principles of behavior theory. The fact that so many excellent teachers "do the right thing naturally" leads to the thought that no approach other than behavior theory in psychological literature seems to agree so completely with various bits of "folk-wisdom."

We will now turn to a more dynamic analysis of the sorts of behaviors dealt with by the classroom teacher.

PROBLEMS OF THE TEACHER

5

Whenever an operant conditioning program is undertaken, the first procedure is to designate carefully the target behavior that is to be developed or eliminated. It is here that the novice in behavior modification may make a serious error. What often happens is that the teacher describes what she *thinks* is happening, and in the process infers motives. For example, a teacher recently asked us how she should work with a high school girl who was resentful and thought she was superior to the teacher. Resentfulness and superiority are inferences by the teacher and not behaviors as such. More accurate descriptions would be that a student talks without permission, writes notes to others, or fails to get homework assignments completed on time. Unseen inner processes such as "resentfulness" may not even exist and, if taken seriously, may be extremely misleading. The actual behavior must be the concern of the teacher.

The teacher should begin any remediation program with proper behavioral designations, both in terms of behaviors observed and behaviors desired. We have sometimes found it helpful to advise a "subscripting" exercise, in which teachers fill in subscripts on a standard diagram for operant reinforcement in this manner:

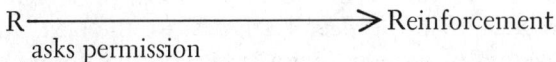

$$R \xrightarrow[\text{asks permission}]{} \text{Reinforcement}$$

The diagram states that the response that we designate "asks permission" leads to reinforcement. Better still, the term S_R is used, this being the standard term for *reinforcing stimulus*. It, too, may be labelled with a subscript, thus:

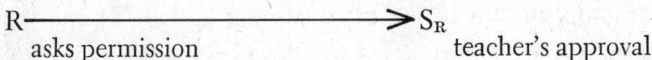

$$R \xrightarrow[\text{asks permission}]{} S_R \atop \text{teacher's approval}$$

It is simpler for a teacher to avoid erroneous inferences about motives if she practices saying "the behavior: (naming it)" in referring to actual and desired behavior patterns. This may seem inconsequential, but the designation of inferred states of mind rather than specific behaviors can render a behavior-modification program meaningless.

We can place problems involving operant behavior into two main categories. First, there are *behavior excesses*, in which certain aspects of the environment reinforce and thereby maintain undesirable operant patterns. Second, there are *behavior deficits*, in which desired patterns for some reason have not been conditioned. Often what seems at first to be a deficit will, on closer examination, prove to be a conditioned operant pattern that gains attention or some other reinforcement. In this section we will consider a number of different problems that have been dealt with in the classroom.

Behavior Excesses

Many teachers use a direct and forceful approach to classroom behavior problems, issuing orders and stating to the children specifically what is to be done and what is not. Subsequently, they single out the violators and give reprimands and further commands. A body of data has begun to accumulate that shows that what often happens is the exact opposite of the predicted effect.

An interesting experiment was performed with a typical class in a school in the lower economic section of a small city. For two weeks an experimenter observed through a mirror-window while the teacher controlled the class in her ordinary manner. Base rates (pretreatment measures) were taken of various undesirable behaviors. Several obvious behaviors were selected for measurement, such as spontaneous talking, whispering to other children, pestering others, gross physical movements, aggressive acts, and being out of the seat. After base rates had been established, the teacher began the second phase of the experiment by writing the "rules" of the classroom on the blackboard. She listed the behaviors upon which the base rates were established, and announced that those were actions that would not be tolerated in the class. Each day, for the next two weeks, the teacher's first action of the morning was to write the forbidden behaviors on the blackboard. During the day the teacher immediately scolded any violation of the rules that she observed. The experimenters meanwhile continued to monitor what was going on in the room. Analysis of the data showed a sharp increase in the rates of the forbidden behaviors soon after the teacher began to pay close attention to them. The teacher noticed the great increase in unruliness; her explanation was that the class must have

gotten "unhappy" with her because of her mood. The experimenters, however, maintained that the systematic attention was having the effect of
reinforcing the forbidden behaviors. This has often been found to be true
of mild, supposedly aversive reprimands and scolding, *particularly with
children who gain very little of the teacher's attention in any other way.*
Some years ago a clinical psychologist pointed out that most children would
rather be punished than be ignored. That, in essence, was the process
going on with some of the children in the classroom just described. A
preferable approach, if the teacher can find any redeeming ability or
achievement in a child, is to build upon it through reinforcement and to
withdraw attention from undesirable behaviors.

In the case just described, the teacher made the remark that the children were possibly rebelling against her mood. There is evidence that
suggests that this is not an adequate explanation. Investigators found that
reprimands for a *single type* of undesirable behavior caused the increase of
only that behavior. For example, the teacher immediately met out-of-seat
behavior with the command, "Sit down, _____," using the child's name.
As the day progressed, the rate of out-of-seat behavior rose higher and
higher. There was very little change, however, in the rates of other undesirable behaviors that were not getting such consistent attention.

Extinction

If behavior excesses exist because they have been reinforced, it
follows that the most direct way to modify the behavior is to reverse the
process by withdrawing reinforcement. Each time an operant behavior is
emitted and is not reinforced, the strength or rate of that particular behavior is reduced. The process is called operant *extinction.* In a systematically
carried out extinction program, the frequency of the operant behavior
becomes lower and lower, until it eventually ceases. In order to appreciate
the potential of extinction for the modification of behavior, we should
realize that extinction refers not only to the withholding of reinforcement
for behaviors that *we* have reinforced in the past, but also to the modification of behaviors reinforced by others in other settings.

An eleven-year-old boy John was far behind his group in spelling ability. When asked to go to the blackboard to spell a word from the daily
spelling exercise, John made faces, mumbled, and stood idle for long periods of time. The initial attempt at spelling always produced little more
than gibberish. The teacher, using the techniques in which she had been
trained, diagnosed the problem as a failure in earlier grades to learn
reading by a phonics method. For this reason she was in the habit of
spending many minutes at a time, when John was at the blackboard, in

efforts to help him "sound out" syllables. The result, after five to ten minutes per word, was usually an eventually correct spelling. Despite the extra time and effort on the teacher's part, John's spelling ability did not improve. Even with the same words, tested a day or so later, John's performance was no better than it had been initially.

A behavior-modification consultant hypothesized that the extra teacher attention might be maintaining the behavior. Treatment began by having the boy go to the blackboard to take a quiz with ten spelling words. The first word was given, and the teacher said, "You work on it until I tell you that it's right." John misspelled the word nearly twenty times. Each time he misspelled, he looked at the teacher, but she seemed engrossed in paperwork on her desk. From the corner of her eye, however, she observed John's progress. Finally John succeeded in spelling the first word, although he had received no prompting or "syllable sounding." At that point the teacher quickly gave him attention and generous praise. Then the second word was given, and a somewhat similar unfolding of events followed. During the first list of ten words, John required fewer and fewer attempts before achieving the correct spelling, and the time involved in arriving at the correct spelling of each successive word was reduced further. In subsequent days the teacher continued the general technique of withdrawing attention from inappropriate behaviors while reinforcing success. After a few weeks John's spelling was up to the average for his grade level, and his various peculiar behaviors at the blackboard (mumbling, pausing, making faces) had vanished. It should be noted that his behavior excess might easily have been mistaken for a behavior deficit.

In a nursery school setting, the frequent crying of some children was the target behavior selected for modification. There seem to be two types of crying, one being a part of a respondent pattern to simuli such as severe pain, and the other being essentially operant. Many children quickly learn to use a tumble or a social rejection as a "reason" to cry when such crying is typically followed by adult attention and comforting. In the nursery school where the research was carried out, the experimenter decided to ignore crying unless it was suspected that the child had experienced an actual physical injury. The teachers' attention and involvement were given only to noncrying children. The teachers soon noted that when crying was not rewarded, children quickly stopped crying and entered into group activities again. The result of the new procedure, after only a few days, was that crying episodes decreased from a typical rate of around ten per morning to zero or one.

Aggression is not frequently thought of as an operant pattern, and indeed it often appears to be a respondent behavior brought about by frustration or the actions of some tormentor. There are many cases, however, in which aggression is clearly maintained as an operant by the attention it receives, or by the submission of others.

Attention is given to aggression, for example, when parents or teachers take a child aside and talk to him individually about his actions. In one school setting, however, attention was removed from the acts of aggression of one particularly troublesome child; instead, the *victim* was quickly joined by the teacher who led him away while conversing on some unrelated topic. The aggressive child, at such times, received no remark or even a glance. On the other hand, any positive social behavior such as cooperation with another child on the part of the aggressive child quickly received the attention and approval of the teacher. Two weeks of such treatment reduced acts of both physical and verbal aggression to less than one-third of their original rates. The results of this experiment might have been even more pronounced, but the actions of teachers from other classes who gave attention to occasional incidents of aggression seem to have maintained aggression to a degree.

With the cases just described, usually two experimental procedures were combined. Attention was not only removed from undesirable behavior, but also delivered for behaviors that were incompatible with the undersirable behavior. *Incompatible* simply means that both behaviors cannot happen at the same time. The most obvious incompatible behavior, though certainly not the only one possible, is whatever is the exact opposite of the behavior in question. Thus, the opposite of social isolation is the approach to, and involvement with, groups. Simple extinction through withdrawal of attention is not nearly as powerful a technique as both extinction and the reinforcement of incompatible patterns.

Behavior Deficits

A *behavior deficit* is a condition in which an individual does not show the social or academic patterns considered appropriate for his age group. The two most likely reasons for a deficit are (1) that the behavior, when emitted, was not reinforced or (2) that the child may not have been around appropriate social models who emitted the behavior in question. In order to appreciate these two factors, let us turn to the question of where operant behavior comes from.

The Sources of Operant Behaviors

There are two sources of operant behaviors. Least important to the educator is *random behavior*, which might strike the observer as "curiosity" or "fooling around." The rate of random activity increases whenever primary drives go unsatisfied. This is why the hungry child is difficult to deal with in the classroom or why a child is restless because of a lack of environmental variety. Random activity, which results sometimes in trial-and-error learning, is of considerable importance to animals in their natural settings and even to human beings who are learning certain movement skills or facing simple mechanical challenges. Of far greater importance to the education of the human being, however, is the fantastically expanded behavioral repertoire offered by the various human models we can observe. *Imitative behavior* is found in all mammal species and is vital to their survival. In man it is the way through which thousands of years of acquired skills are transmitted during a short period in the pupil's early lifetime. The tendency of human beings to imitate is manifested very early in their speech acquisition. Children imitate syllables and eventually simple words that have been slowly sounded out to them— ma-ma, da-da. The parent tends to reinforce certain of these utterances with exclamations of delight and increased attentiveness.

It is difficult to determine the exact degree to which the tendency toward general imitation is itself strengthened through reinforcement. Some persons feel that such a tendency is at least partly innate, but several studies have shown that there are situational factors influencing the degree of imitation.

1. Children more frequently imitate those who are their major agents of reinforcement (usually mother and father).
2. Children more frequently imitate same-sex models.
3. Children more frequently imitate high-status individuals within their peer groups.
4. Children more frequently imitate behaviors that they are able to see lead to reinforcement of some aspect of another person's behavior (sometimes called *vicarious reinforcement*).

There is no question regarding children's tendency to pick up behavior patterns—even prejudices—that are practiced by those with whom they associate. These behaviors are emitted during the general term of interaction with others and, if reinforced, become part of the persisting pattern of conditioned habits. A knowledge of these influences upon children's behavior is valuable, so that we can best set up conditions in the classroom. We should attempt to provide the proper imitative influences in order that the children might emit the specific target behaviors we seek and thereby make those behaviors available for teacher-reinforcement. It is possible to place children into a designed project group, made up of certain selected individuals, to maximize such developments.

The potential effect of peer-group behaviors and patterns of peer reinforcement may be illustrated by means of an interesting study performed some years ago with college students. A number of students at a Deep South university and at a North Central university were involved. At the Northern university a group of in-state resident students were compared with some Southern students on a racial prejudice scale. At the Southern university a group of Northern students was found and compared with resident students on the same scale.

As freshmen, the Northern students at the Northern university were very similar to the Northern students at the Southern university—low in total points on the prejudice scale. Similarly, both groups of Southern students were high on the scale, with those entering the school in the North little different from those attending the Southern school.

In the senior year, the original individuals who were still enrolled were again measured. Their prejudice scores as seniors were compared with their scores as freshmen. Both of the out-of-state groups who were attending schools in a different geographic region showed major changes in the direction of their university peer group. The Southern students at the Northern university had practically the same scores, as seniors, as did the Northern students at the same school. Similarly, the Northern students who went South to school became quite prejudiced.

The important aspect of this study is that racial prejudice is a characteristic of some human beings that is resistant to change to a dismaying degree. A number of films that are often used in the elementary schools and are intended to reduce such attitudes are quite popular with teachers, but what research there is suggests that they have practically no effect in changing the behaviors of the children who view them. In all the psychological literature, there have only been one or two procedures that have been shown to radically affect racial attitudes. The case just described illustrates one of these procedures—the powerful effect of peer-group attitudes on the individual when the individual depends upon the group for day-to-day social reinforcement. The careful placement of the individual problem-child into a predesigned social group can, under the proper circumstances, almost itself remediate a number of stubborn problems.

Examples of Deficits

It is easiest to begin this topic by describing some problems that are *not* specifically tied in with classroom achievement. A case recently came to our attention in which a mentally retarded five-year-old child had not acquired speech. The parents, as is often true in cases involving handicapped youngsters, passed off the deficit as due to the handicap and had expected scarcely any productive behavior from their child. In this case, however, we observed that when the child wanted to be picked up, or wanted food or a drink of water, he gestured in some manner, grunted, and then began a mixed pattern of gesturing and screaming while the parents ran about trying to supply him with what they guessed was his desire. The parents had picked up some skill at recognizing the gestures and even interpreting the tones of the screaming in terms of what motivated it. Our hypothesis was that the child found it easiest not to bother with speech and was being reinforced quite adequately without it.

Treatment in this case began by terminating the parents' usual response to the grunts, screams, and gestures. As if he were a one-year-old, the appropriate word was slowly sounded out to the boy, and he had to emit a reasonable imitation of "water," "pick up," and so forth before he gained his objective. Within a day the boy had established some crude speech patterns that had obviously been within his capabilities for some time. By not having to emit complex speech patterns in the home, this child had taken a "lazy" route to the satisfaction of his wants. Parents' too frequent tendency to fatalistically write off handicapped children's incapacities results in such children seldom achieving the levels that they might otherwise reach. The lesson in this case is not limited to handicapped children. Neither parents nor teachers should assume that because a child is "introverted," "immature," and so forth, he therefore cannot be expected to interact, cooperate, and achieve.

Many, if not most, behavior deficits are mixtures of deficits with behavior excesses. A case in point involves a published account of a nursery school child who crawled about on hands and knees most of the time. Two hypotheses advanced by the staff were (1) that she was not capable of walking because of lack of practice or some physical limitation or (2) that she was "regressed" in a Freudian sense. According to the latter interpretation, she adopted an infantile pattern in an effort to reexperience the emotional gratifications of her earlier life. Both these hypotheses were refuted by subsequent procedures. By simply placing desirable objects on tables and giving great amounts of attention to the child whenever she raised herself to an on-feet position to get them, the staff rapidly increased the amount of her on-feet behavior, including walking, until it occupied most of her day. Obviously it was necessary to concurrently ignore the child, almost as if she were invisible, whenever she was in an off-feet position. The reader will notice at this point how easy it is to designate behavior properly—in this case off-feet versus on-feet.

Another case of mixed excess and deficit was also in a nursery school. Social isolation was the target behavior selected for remediation. Social isolates make up only a small percentage of the children in a typical nursery school, but their behaviors are usually of great concern to the teacher. Isolates are typically found outside of the play area, or on its fringes, and the few approaches they make toward others are usually toward adults.

Typically such children seek a continuous one-to-one interaction with an adult. The adult's most frequent response to such a child is comfort and reassurance, which reinforces the behavior. In one class where such a child had been enrolled for several weeks, the teacher began to involve herself only with group activities, and disengaged from all contacts with single individuals. She took notice, without direct looks, of the isolate child. Whenever the child made any movement toward the group, the teacher looked directly at her with a broad smile, then redirected her attention to the group. During the first morning of this procedure, the child occasionally entered the group's activities when the group was quiet and engrossed in something, and at such times she received close, affectionate attention from the group-involved teacher. Gradually, over several days, the rate of group interaction for the isolate child increased until it was at the level of the class average. During the last two days of the program, the teacher spent less and less time in close interaction with the group, disengaging shortly after the involvement of the isolate child. The interaction rate of the child continued at the level that had been attained, an outcome suggesting that the interaction in group activity itself had become reinforcing to her.

In another case an eleven-year-old boy demonstrated "social immaturity," which, among other things, included giggling, occasional tantrums, and generally disruptive classroom behavior. The teacher began her program by ignoring the behavior. Only when the boy seemed to be listening attentively in class did she act. The boy, at such times, was asked a question that he could usually answer, with the result that he received praise. Even when he did not know the answer, he at least gained a nice smile from the teacher if he had not shown an undesirable behavior. Prior to this time the boy was far behind in his academic achievement. For the first time in the year, he began to make good progress, and the rate of his immature behavior fell off drastically. Both the extinction of immature behaviors and reinforcement of mature ones were involved in this case.

The degree of change of severe behavior problems that is usually produced through techniques such as those just described seems unbelievable to many experienced teachers. Under a normal routine or in an inconsistently carried-out behavior modification program, it is unusual to see such rapid and major remediation. The key to gaining such results lies in the absolute necessity of *ignoring* the child when he is not emitting acceptable behaviors. Total and complete ignoring is not something that many children choose to endure for very long.

For those who are interested in further studies of social deficits and their treatments, the professional literature contains many cases. Most of these are in special settings for mentally retarded children, but other cases have been published. Suggestions for further reading will be presented later on.

Academic Deficits

In cases in which the deficit is in academically directed behaviors, we assume that the motivating conditions have not been adequate to keep the child achieving to normative standards. If effective education for such children is to continue, it is best to go back to the level of actual achievement shown by each child and begin from there with the programs of individualized instruction, using reinforcement procedures. Parents often approximate this procedure when they bring a tutor into their home. Tutors are seldom as experienced and skillful as the child's own classroom teacher. Nevertheless, the usual result is that the child makes accelerated progress. The reason is simple. A very large proportion of the child's correct responses gain reinforcement in the tutor's presence—a condition that seldom exists in the typical large classroom. The alert classroom teacher can increase her effectiveness with individual children by concentrating quantities of attention and approval on the achieving child. By "achieving" child, we mean *all* who achieve at any rate, including slower students. All children should be recognized for the progress they make. The first and probably most difficult step is for the teacher to concentrate her attention on desired rather than undesired behaviors in the classroom. This can be done with individual children in a variety of ingenious ways that any skillful teacher can devise. Again, it is necessary to carefully designate the behaviors the teacher wishes to develop. Two comments are offered here, which have occurred to many readers:

1. The behaviors should eventually be defined more in terms of products than efforts. Only in the early stages of a classroom program should a child be reinforced for simply sitting still and looking at something on his desk. (One expert terms this the "dead man test.")
2. Products such as correct arithmetic achievement should gain as conspicuous social reinforcement as poster preparation or art work that teachers frequently post on classroom walls for all to see. The teacher, if she feels that arithmetic achievement is desirable and should be developed, should be prepared to give consistent reinforcement for each child's correct daily processing of assigned problems.

There is much that the classroom teacher can do without great difficulty to increase the academic achievement of individual members of her class. She will gain more knowledge of the systematic development of the operant behaviors of individuals in Chapter 6, and about total-class strategies in Chapter 8.

Summary

1. Teachers should be very clear about identifying children's behaviors in terms of *actual fact* and should avoid guesses at motives or intentions.
2. Identification of behaviors should specify behavior deficits, which are usually treated through reinforcement programs, and behavior excesses, which are treated through extinction and reinforcement of incompatible patterns of behavior.
3. The teacher should be aware of the powerful effects, on behavior, of the actions and reinforcers provided by the peer group. Imitative influences can be used in constructive ways in the remediation of problems.

ADDITIONAL OPERANT PRINCIPLES

6

In this section we shall consider some of the finer points of the principles and techniques that are important to the effective operation of a classroom behavior-modification program.

Immediate Reinforcement

Reinforcement must be *immediate* if it is to succeed. Many studies have confirmed the fact that even a ten- or fifteen-second delay in reinforcement is too great for effective conditioning. Moreover, the reinforcing effect is associated with whatever behavior is ongoing during the moment immediately preceding the onset of the reinforcer. A delay of more than a few seconds often results in the diversion of a child's attention from the work he was doing to some other behavior. If a child completes a task, sits half a minute, and begins to daydream, then gets a reinforcer, it is daydreaming rather than on-task behavior that will increase in its subsequent frequency.

Percentage of Reinforcement

The percentage of reinforcement is an extremely important aspect of a behavior-modification program. So far we have discussed reinforcement as if it were necessary or desirable to reinforce each and every instance of an emitted behavior that we are trying to strengthen.

The establishment and the maintenance of a behavior can be viewed as two independent procedures. The establishment of a behavior should begin with a close-to-100-percent schedule of reinforcement. That is, *each time* the behavior is emitted, it should be reinforced if at all possible. This is called continuous reinforcement. In this manner a high rate of behavior can be most quickly established. However, it is scarcely possible to use continuous reinforcement schedules permanently in a classroom, nor is it desirable. Behavior maintained on a continuous (100 percent) schedule of reinforcement extinguishes much more rapidly when reinforcement is withheld than does behavior maintained on a partial schedule of reinforcement. Therefore, once behavior is beginning to be satisfactorily established, the percentage of reinforcement given to that behavior should be progressively "thinned." Eventually, if done in a gradual manner, a 5 to 10 percent rate of reinforcement can satisfactorily maintain the behavior, as well as give it considerable resistance to extinction.

Case

Many experimenters get the best results by making successive, thinned-out reinforcers larger. In a state school for mentally retarded youngsters, a twelve-year-old boy was in the habit of urinating and defecating in his trousers several times a day. Social rejection and occasional assaults by his peers who said he "smelled" had had no effect on the behavior, nor had conventional attempts at toilet training. The staff physicians expressed the opinion that structural brain damage connected with the condition of retardation had made it impossible for the boy to gain physical control over his evacuative functions.

Money was considered to be a good reinforcer in that setting, as patronage of a snack bar and the commissary required payments of cash. The experimenter told the twelve-year-old that he would be checked three times a day to see if he had soiled himself. Each time, if he was clean, he would receive a nickel. The boy was much improved during the first four days of the program, being soiled only twice of the twelve times when inspected. Thereafter he was offered no more nickels, but a dime after the third daily inspection, provided that the results of all three inspections were satisfactory. The dime phase lasted for seven days, during which time there were no accidents. Then the procedure called for one daily inspection, with a quarter as reward at the end of the week if there had been no soiling. The quarter phase lasted for seven weeks, during which time there was only one accident, which came about while the child was upset by a scolding about a rule infraction. The results of this case, while appearing simple, are impressive when one considers the twelve-year history of failure to develop proper toilet habits and the tremendous amount of past effort in that direction. In this case reinforcers were thinned out, but the size of each reinforcer was increased. Meanwhile the initial cost of $1.05 per week decreased to $0.25.

Negative Reinforcement

So far we have considered reinforcers only in the nature of rewards. The acquisition of rewards, which we have merely called "reinforcement," is more accurately termed *positive* reinforcement. There is another way, however, in which behavior may be reinforced. In this process a behavior succeeds in reducing or eliminating an aversive, unpleasant condition. Such escape results in the strengthening, by *negative* reinforcement, of the behavior that brought it about. This concept explains the acquisition of a great number of stress-related habit patterns.

Example

In one classroom, a nine-year-old girl Laura became upset when she had to participate in classwork. She would become sick and typically would vomit in the classroom. Whenever she did, she was allowed to leave the class to lie down. By the time she felt better, the class had usually ended. Although severe emotional upset is capable of producing respondent-type vomiting, the regularity of the behavior as well as the teacher's response to it created the suspicion that Laura's case was one of operant vomiting, maintained by escape from an aversive situation. The teacher was advised to move the child to a different section of the classroom after she vomited so that the area could be cleaned, to tell Laura that she was sorry she was sick and hoped that she felt better soon, and to continue with the lessons with Laura in the room. By withdrawing negative reinforcement, vomiting was quickly eliminated.

Limitations of the Use of Negative Reinforcement

Negative reinforcement is the manner in which many behaviors—both appropriate and inappropriate—are developed and maintained. In certain clinical settings negative reinforcement has been deliberately used in behavior modification, but its use in the educational setting is not ordinarily advised. In order to allow escape from an aversive stimulus, that stimulus first has to be presented. This would pair the aversive circumstance with the school, the subject matter, and the teacher, and could produce emotional side-effects through classical conditioning. There will be a discussion of this topic in the next section. It is enough at this point to understand that it often becomes necessary to recognize and remove the opportunity for undesirable negative reinforcement, as in the example of Laura's vomiting habit.

Shaping

The literature of behavior modification contains many references to the shaping of behavior. In shaping, one sets a standard for the child's performance, and reinforcement comes only when the performance meets the standard. The standard remains unchanged until the child's behavior is consistently gaining reinforcement, at which time it is raised. The child must then increase the level or precision of his performance in order to continue to gain reinforcement. This is a simple procedure, easily observed in the acquisition of social skills, ability to pronounce words, development of various academic abilities, and the like. This procedure, if carefully used, can result in high levels of skillful behaviors that often bear little resemblance, at the end, to the early behaviors that gained reinforcement. Frequent shortcomings in shaping attempts are:

1. Setting too high standards at the outset, which results in few reinforcements and the child's discouragement.
2. Moving the standard up before the response pattern begins to consistently meet the preceding standard.
3. Moving the standard up too far in a single step.
4. Finally settling for a level of precision that is far below the child's ultimate potential.

The procedure of shaping lies at the heart of academic development in which students build upon initial skills as their education continues, as with mathematics and spelling. Laboratory experiments with simple tasks are yielding a great deal of knowledge that shows, among other things, why some children—particularly in certain teachers' classrooms—fall further and further behind the rest of the class.

In many cases, point number two, cited in the preceding list, is violated. Not too long ago we looked at a sixth-grade procedure in spelling instruction. Using a workbook, each child had several opportunities to write out the words on the week's spelling list. One of the first things I noticed was that some children's workbooks were not filled in, but that is a secondary point at the moment. The critical shortcoming was that after a certain amount of assumed practice, the children took a quiz, which was the termination of their involvement with the week's word list. In other words, the children's quiz papers showed all of the various words that they did not know how to spell, but no further effort was made to teach those words. Perhaps the reader—a busy classroom teacher—will now say, "I just can't possibly follow up each of my forty children on their individual mistakes," but there are ways of doing just that. One teacher of my acquaintance enlists the children themselves, after spelling quizzes, to tutor and test each other until the missing gaps in learning are filled in.

It would be profitable for all teachers who employ any form of class-room reinforcement procedure to go over the four common shortcomings in shaping, in an effort to analyze their own practices that may come under that heading.

Chaining

Where shaping refers to unitary or global behaviors, there are a large number of behaviors that are not unitary at all, but consist of a *chain* of many smaller units of behavior. Each unit in the chain is emitted in a fixed sequence. Examples are bicycle riding, walking, tying a tie or shoe-lace, saying the months of the year and the letters of the alphabet, and the like. Chaining is based on the fact that many behaviors are learned within the context of preceding behaviors. Because of a cue, of which one may or may not be fully aware, one makes a response. The response then gives further cues that cause further responses. Take away the opportunity of emitting some early or intermediate response, and without the resulting cue further units in the chain become quite difficult to emit properly. For example, if one asks a child to say what letter of the alphabet follows *q*, he is likely to begin, "*a, b, c, d, . . . ,*" until he arrives at "*. . . o, p,*" which then gives the cue for the next letter in the chain. It is necessary for the child to produce *behaviors* that serve as stimuli for further behaviors. Most of the literature on chaining is quite recent and seems so far to have emphasized motor learning. There do seem to be some interesting princi-ples, however, that may have the potential for expediting the educational processes where chained units are concerned. For example, it has been shown in laboratories that chaining proceeds much more rapidly if one learns the last unit in the chain first, then the last two units together, and so forth. Recently an experimental programmed instruction unit in our laboratory school taught youngsters to do long division by presenting almost-worked-through problems, which the students had to complete. Gradually the amount left incomplete was increased until the students were working entire problems. The teacher's report was that the principles of long division were learned more rapidly than with the usual procedures and with less confusion at intermediate points along the way.

We also know from the established principles of chaining that, where errors are made in a chain of behaviors, the individual should go back be-yond the error before working forward again. For example, if a child en-ters the house, sheds his jacket, and throws it onto a chair, the parent should not tell him to pick it up and hang it. The child should be told to put on the coat, go out again, reenter, and then remove the coat and hang it properly. In this way initial behaviors become cues only to proper subse-quent behaviors in the child's habit structure. Since most classroom learning occurs within a larger context of knowledge, the same principles should apply to the restructuring of the situation when homework or quizzes are reviewed and corrected or when static items of information are given in class in response to students' questions. It is best to have the student actually go through the process of using the unit of information correctly in the larger context of which it is a part.

The next few years will undoubtedly produce important findings on chaining that will have direct applications to the classroom. Using the findings based on the chaining phenomenon, we may even find out something about such mysterious functions as "meaning," "thinking," and "reasoning," all of which appear to involve chained associations. If nothing else, knowledge of the chaining phenomenon is of importance for full appreciation of the prompt-and-fade method, which is the next topic of discussion.

Prompting and Fading

Some yars ago it occurred to some psychologists that classroom learning often involves a great deal of "error practicing." Suppose that a child is asked to state the product of 8 × 8, but because of his weak habit structure he answers 54. He not only has given a wrong answer, but also has practiced an error association—a linking of 8 × 8 with 54. Experimenters have developed what has become known as "errorless discrimination learning," which has been successfully employed in some of the programmed instruction units on the market. Essentially, it was found that people learn more quickly if they can be prevented from practicing errors during learning. Programmed instruction usually achieves this to a degree by making a simple statement and then asking the student for immediate responses that involve elements of the statement. Additional complexity is added only gradually. The prompt-and-fade method, additionally, gives the student enough of a hint to insure that he can complete the entire answer without error. For example, "The sixteenth United States president was Abraham L_____." As sessions progress, less and less of the prompt is given. By gradually fading out the prompt, one achieves perfect learning with no error practice. The procedure can be swift and sure, depending of course on the care and precision of the teacher. This method is only beginning to be systematically employed in the classroom.

Differential Reinforcement

Differential reinforcement simply means the reinforcement of some behaviors and not others from the total behavioral repertoire. A great deal of what we often assume is some highly abstract process, like the development of "maturity," is simply the product of differential reinforcement. The development of conversation in the child often involves this procedure. We typically reinforce meaningful attempts at conversation, while we extinguish butting in, shrieking, or meaningless babble by withdrawing from the interaction when they occur. Soon we see that the child shows "increased maturity," in that he converses more nicely with adults with fewer outbursts. The thoughtful reader may also have recognized that differential reinforcement is involved in the shaping process, as we cease to reinforce patterns that no longer meet our standard but which once gained reinforcement.

Discriminative Conditioning

Discriminative conditioning refers to the development of the child's capacity to act in certain ways *only* at appropriate times. Superficially this seems to involve rational "understanding," but the process is easily demonstrated in very simple animal organisms and is developed through operant conditioning. Suppose that a six-year-old boy behaves very childishly with his grandmother, and his supposed inabilities and requests for help are reinforced by her attention. We say that the grandmother functions as S+, a stimulus in the presence of which the behavior is reinforced. The mother, on the other hand, may serve as S—, a stimulus in the presence of which the behavior is *not* reinforced. Soon the child is able to discriminate between circumstances in which he should emit the behavior and those in which he should not.

In the process of speech development, a great deal of discriminative conditioning occurs. At one point in his early life, the child frequently talks to himself. As people (S+) reinforce such behavior, but no reinforcement occurs when there are no others in the room (S—), we see a greater and greater proportion of the child's speech occurring in the presence of others.

Discriminative conditioning or its absence is involved in the creation of many problem behaviors. One example, involving its absence, is the situation in which some children behave with adults very much as they behave with other children—refusing to obey, "talking back," and in general irritating their elders. In analyzing such cases and preparing for their remediation, it is necessary to recognize that failure to discriminate will come about whenever the child does not have the opportunity to experience *both* S+ and S— and the different consequences for various kinds of responding in the presence of each.

PUNISHMENT

7

To many, the classroom without massive strategies of punishment is inconceivable. In fact the history of education, from its earliest stages to the present, shows a primary reliance on aversive methods of classroom control. Threats are put forth and are often backed up when students are out of line with the classroom regulations. Some classrooms operate in turmoil, with teachers trying to shout down students. Others are armed camps, with students walking a tightrope between what they think the teacher can enforce and what they think she cannot. Many teachers are driven from the field by the difficulties that they encounter in trying to control their classrooms. Even ten years ago, it was reported that inability to cope with classroom behavior problems was the major cause of first-year teachers leaving the profession, particularly at the secondary level. In the past four or five years, there have been further upsurges in student resistance to authority. It is now considered admirable among many youngsters to invoke abstract principles of freedom and self-expression to justify rule violations. Unfortunately, many teachers possess only one technique—punishment—in their control procedures.

Most teachers enter their first teaching experience predisposed, at least to a degree, toward the employment of positive attitudes of friendship and reason in dealing with students. Then, even as early as the end of student teaching, their approach begins to change to that of a tougher, firmer method. Recently a list of classroom-control procedures was compiled by a class of students just back from elementary and secondary student teaching. These tips were, in the words of the assignment, "techniques that work" in maintaining classroom discipline, and presumably each had become popular with at least one of the student teachers. The list contained 128 tips, about 110 of which would be considered punitive. One would be hard put to compose so thorough a list of ways in which to humiliate, insult, and embarrass the dignity of other human beings. We should ask ourselves why there is such reliance on control methods that punish. The answer is very simple—punishment ordinarily has the effect of momentarily stopping whatever outburst that is disturbing the teacher. Teachers can be reinforced too, and here the teacher has emitted a behavior that is negatively reinforced. Because of regular reinforcement, punishing is strengthened in teachers, and once established, such techniques become increasingly ingrained in the teacher's behavior.

An objective discussion of punishment must concern two separate aspects: (1) reasons for and against its use, and (2) the technology of its operation.

Should Punishment Be Employed?

We already know that punishment works, in terms of momentarily stopping undesirable classroom behavior. This effect is of variable duration, depending on the severity of the punishment. The resulting decrease in the rate of the punished behavior is called *suppression*. In recent years it has been popular to perform experiments that show that punished behavior, unlike extinguished behavior, comes back or tends to persist at some low rate. There has probably been an overemphasis on this argument, since some experiments have shown that extremely severe punishment can result in virtually complete and permanent suppression of the punished act. Our emphasis will be on other facts that suggest that punishment not be extensively employed in the classroom.

Emotional Side Effects

Perhaps the most serious result of the continued use of punishment in the classroom is classical conditioning of undesirable emotional states. Frequently punished students are the first to drop out of the educational process. When such students do remain in school, they are the most alienated from teachers and are typically found in the back-row seats, as far from the teacher as they can sit. Low-ability students are frequently punished for the best work of which they are capable. It is understandably difficult for the teacher to judge whether a student is performing to capacity, but the injustice of such punishment, coupled with the frustration that already exists from struggling unsuccessfully with daily school requirements, creates an enduring aversion to education in those of limited ability. Moreover, continued frustration and punishment have both been shown, in laboratories, to elicit a respondent form of aggression. It would appear that the twin goals of keeping such students in the educational setting for as long as possible and reducing aggressive acts against property and persons would justify a movement away from techniques of punishment.

Efficiency of Punishment

Aside from the partly justified claim that the suppression effects from punishment are more temporary than either extinction or the effects from reinforcement of incompatible alternative behaviors that are more desirable, there is another criterion of efficiency that punishment falls short of. Specifically, it derives from the fact that punishment leads to a passive form of learning. Punishment produces an associative link between a behavior and the resulting punishment, but *no* association is formed involving proper behavior. At worst, the child may know what *not* to do, but not know *what* to do or *how* to do it. This contrasts strongly with the differential reinforcement of proper behaviors when they occur in an effort to produce an effectively functioning individual.

Punishment and Academic Achievement

Frequently, the teacher observes that the threat motivation works well in comparison with no plan of motivation at all in a lethargic classroom. As a result, she may reach a hasty conclusion about the desirability of punishment. A large literature has established that emotional upset, such as that brought about by punishment or the anticipation of punishment, is not contributive to complex, patterned learning. The teacher may recall her own "test anxiety" as a student. A similar situation exists in which a child is marginal in ability and fears the examination and the teacher's criticism of the products of his efforts. Anticipation of punishment instills anxiety, and anxiety inhibits complex learning.

The Proper Use of Punishment

Punishment is a useful procedure at certain stages in a child's life. As a general guideline, we can say that punishment *should* be used with persons who cannot be verbally guided toward the proper behavior that can then be reinforced. This criterion obviously applies to infant training, where hands—or even bottoms—are sometimes slapped. With retarded children the criterion might still apply, at least where the target behavior might result in injury to the child or to others, or result in damage to expensive property. With the normal child in the classroom, however, punishment does not ordinarily seem to be the best possible procedure.

If punishment is to be used, there are certain guidelines for its employment. First, mild punishment such as a spoken "no" or "wrong" can have informational value without much attendant emotional arousal. Even this degree of punishment should be focused on cases in which the child needs the emphasis to notice his error. Retarded children, for example, sometimes do better when their every classroom response is met with "right," coupled with praise, or "wrong." We again stress, however, the deemphasis of punishment, both in terms of its severity and duration.

If punishment is to be used, it should occur during or immediately after the target behavior. If there must be more than five or six seconds of delay after the undesirable behavior ceases, punishment might as well be abandoned as a procedure. Only persons skilled in re-creating some sort of "mental image reenactment" of the behavior, which is unreliable at best, can expect any actual behavioral change with delayed punishment.

The teacher should be alert for any sign that the result of the punishment is an increase in the rate of the punished behavior. As indicated in Chapter 5, there are children who seek attention so desperately that even a scolding functions as a positive reinforcer for them. Such children present no special problem once the teacher recognizes the true nature of the situation, as they usually are more responsive than the other children in a class to the more positive forms of attention.

Time-Out from Positive Reinforcement

In most existing behavior-modification programs, *time-out* is administered when the child's behavior is harmful or disturbing to others. The procedure involves the child being quietly and gently removed, without scolding or any other undue attention, and he is placed in a time-out area. Where children are working toward rewards (see Chapter 8), time-out procedures remove the child from the setting, and he cannot achieve and earn. If the setting is free time in a play area, the child is removed and cannot continue in the fun. With well-socialized small children it is often enough to have them sit on the floor in the back of the room for five or ten minutes. Problem children who are unduly rebellious can be taken to a time-out room, which should be a small, empty room where there is nothing to look at and nothing to do, and which can be locked from the outside. Some administrators are reluctant to authorize a time-out room, although it is not entirely understandable why they should object to this quiet and relatively dignified alternative to an emotion-packed public disciplinary scene which leaves all concerned visibly upset. The teacher who employs time-out procedures would be well advised to avoid thinking of it as punishment. A hot or dark closet or long periods of time-out should not be employed. The purpose of time-out from positive reinforcement is simply to bore the student, so that he will be happy to get back to classroom activities.

Many experts do not classify time-out as punishment, since punishment is usually defined as the *infliction* of an aversive stimulus. Time-out *removes* attractive stimuli for a short time. Time-out is virtually the only consequence to undesirable behavior in token economy settings, which are described in the next chapter.

Which Motivation To Use?

It seems that there are about three general forms of motivational strategy that are employed in classroom: (1) an emphasis on positive reinforcement, (2) an emphasis on negative reinforcement and punishment, and (3) no motivational plan at all—just classroom progression through material so as to keep on a schedule or timetable. Surely by this time it can be seen that the writer's sympathies lie with the first alternative. We might point out right now that many teachers involve their children in a large number of "fun" projects, avoid homework assignments, and generally keep the students happy in ways that do not subscribe to the real meaning of positive reinforcement. A characteristic of a well-run program emphasizing positive reinforcement is that there is considerable progress in the class and the "fun" comes as a reward for actual achievement.

SOPHISTICATED OPERANT CONTROL
The Token Economy

8

Direct reinforcement of behavior, as we have shown, can be a powerful force for change. Usually a direct reinforcement program concerns a single target behavior. Where problems are specific, such programs can be highly effective. Many behaviors, however, are neither simple nor specific. They are highly patterned, and the "correct" act may show considerable variety from one time to the next. Academic achievement is such a pattern. Here, a flexible means of reinforcement is highly desirable. Similarly, the social interactions of problem groups such as maladjusted or retarded children and the like are patterns of considerable complexity. Here too, flexible techniques should be employed.

Tokens

Some years ago a chimpanzee was taught to work for plastic poker chips that could be exchanged for raisins in a slot machine. Gradually the animal was brought to the point of working through an entire day, saving his chips in order to spend them in the evening. This is a classic experiment in the literature of conditioned reinforcement. The poker chips are what we would call tokens.

A *token* is a tangible item having no value of its own, which is given as a payment and which can be exchanged at specific times for items that do have value. In token exchange programs the items of value that are indirectly acquired are called back-up reinforcers. A token program becomes a *token economy* if a wide range of behaviors are paid off with tokens and if a large number of effective items and privileges are employed as the back-up reinforcers. In many institutional settings the token economy is so complete that *all* desirable things must be purchased with tokens.

Advantages of Token Economies

There are a number of advantages offered by token programs. Among them are:

1. No *satiation effect*. Satiation can be a problem if primary reinforcers are employed. If a child works for candy, he stops working when he has had enough. Trinkets, which offer environmental variety, show a similar satiation effect.
2. No *extinction effect*. Extinction can be a problem if social reinforcers are employed. Praise and, to a lesser extent, attention "wear out" if used too frequently.
3. No *distraction effect*. Children do not stop to consume tokens, as they do food reinforcers, nor do they pay much attention to tokens, which have little amusement value.
4. *Flexible administration*. Tokens can be offered for all the behaviors the teacher chooses to develop. Also, the payoff rate can be adjusted to reflect the amount of the student's time and effort involved in the behavior.
5. *Flexible redemption*. An effective token system offers a wide variety of back-up reinforcers for the student's choice. What is reinforcing for one child may not be for another. Even with only one child, what is highly reinforcing for him on one day may be met with indifference the next.
6. *Control over children who are unresponsive to social reinforcers*. Tokens have proved to be powerful influences on children who seemed "unreachable" in conventional ways. Also, pairings of token presentation with attention and approval develops receptivity to those social reinforcers.
7. *Little delay of reinforcement*. Tokens are given out at the moment of achievement. This is in contrast to grades on report cards, which involve a great deal of delay.
8. Finally, over a period of time a token economy can *develop a sensitivity* to the existence of behavior-reinforcement contingencies (see next section).

Creating Sensitivity to Contingencies

The average adult is highly influenced by elaborate systems of social and token exchanges. Individuals detect approval or disapproval of their actions and adjust their behaviors accordingly, remaining alert for subsequent evaluations of their behavior by others. Even the typical young child has developed an appreciable, although not particularly subtle, system of social exchange patterns by the time he begins his formal schooling.

Very young children often show attentiveness and a remarkable sensitivity to their mother's reactions to their behaviors. This ability is best described as a sensitivity to the typical behavior-reinforcment contingencies. It comes about within a framework of parental discipline and consistency in responding to the child's actions.

Sensitivity to behavior-reinforcement contingencies is deficient, at least to a degree, in most mentally retarded youngsters. These children need to have very obvious consequences to their behaviors repeatedly stressed. The consistency and immediacy of the token reinforcement environment is excellent for them.

Some children of normal intelligence and alertness grow up in environments that do not foster such sensitivity. Most of these children's homes can no doubt be called inadequate, where the children run wild and succeed at various personal indulgences. There are many other homes that outwardly appear excellent but where children are taken care of in much the same manner as laboratory animals. That is, the children's actions have little influence on the treatment of them by their parents. Some of these homes may seem emotionally cold, while others may appear indulgent and loving. In essence, though, there are no differential consequences to the child for his different styles of behavior. A remarkable number of society's problems can be traced to this form of child rearing. These include many instances of aggression against adults, fighting, bullying, tantrums, obscenity, and other self-indulgent behaviors. The behavior of the child eventually goes through transition into adult patterns of a similar nature. Most assault charges in our courts are against adults who, as children, were allowed to aggress without clear-cut differential consequences. Such children's rule-violations never actually had any consistent effect upon the reinforcers they received. This style of child rearing, in its many forms, is perhaps the main factor behind the lack of responsibility seen so often in developing young adults. Often the parents, who are responsible, look to the classroom teacher for remediation.

Case

In the fall of 1968, ten children were removed from fourth-grade classrooms in a large university laboratory school because of severe disciplinary infractions. A plan for a special experimental token economy classroom was presented to the school's principal. The principal, who had little idea of how a token economy system operated, had been intending to have the children completely removed from the school. He welcomed any possibility of keeping them, so long as their customary troublemaking could be brought under some degree of control. The principal made the facilities of the school available to the experimenters on a flexible basis.

It was the fourth week of school, in October, when the ten children were brought into the class. They were all different, one from another, but alike in their school history. Each had been disturbing his class by participating in one or several disruptive behaviors. They spoke out without permission, shouted, were out of their seats frequently, verbally abused others, screamed, struck, or kicked other children, and had tantrums. Most of their time was spent in paying attention to other children in the class instead of the teacher. Susan, according to the school records, was given to lying on the floor and kicking when she could not have her way. Chris had tearful tantrums, followed on occasion by hours of sobbing. Moreover, nine of the ten children were classified by the school as "slow learners." It was not known to what degree their behavioral problems were actually responsible, rather than lack of ability.

On the first day of class the token economy was explained. The fourth-grade academic subjects had been broken down into rigidly sequenced and numbered exercise sheets, with instructions for working the exercises and examples, where necessary, written out at the top. These exercise sheets had been developed by a team of elementary teachers and covered all the academic material usually presented during the fourth-grade year.

There were no lectures or demonstrations. Each day the class began with each child being given an exercise sheet. The child worked until finished with the sheet and then took it directly to the teacher, who checked the answer boxes on the child's sheet against a key. Token payment was made only for a score of 90 or 100 percent correct, depending upon the type of exercise. The accuracy requirement for payment as well as the token value of the sheet was clearly marked in an upper corner. If a child's sheet did not meet the accuracy standard, the teacher kept the sheet and issued a duplicate sheet with the items missed checked for special attention. The student then returned to his seat and completed the entire sheet again. On rare occasions when a child showed a persisting error pattern, the teacher spent a few minutes quietly pointing out the principles involved in problems of that type. As soon as a child completed an exercise sheet, he was praised, given the appropriate number of "points," and given a new exercise sheet of the teacher's choice.

Before proceeding, the following facts deserve notice in the procedure we have described. (1) This was individualized instruction, with the teacher "prescribing" the exact subject matter that she felt was indicated for each child. (2) The child had only one task—to complete the answer boxes with a high level of accuracy. No other behaviors earned him any points. (3) In order to complete the answer boxes, the child had to read the directions and examples carefully, and work carefully on the problems. Hasty, error-filled work earned no points. (4) Each child could progress under this system as rapidly as his ability allowed. (5) No child was held back by slower members of the group, as is usual with the lecture-demonstration method. (6) Unlike most "workbook" programs, the procedures in this case were designed to generate enthusiasm by immediately rewarding achievement.

Back-up reinforcers went beyond material rewards such as the candy and entertainment items typical in most token systems. The emphasis in this case was upon *non*material rewards. At specified times the children could spend their tokens, if they had enough, on recess, double-length recess, feeding the three caged animals in the classroom, hot lunch in the cafeteria, dessert after lunch, playground privileges after lunch, being teacher's assistant and helping grade others' exercise sheets under supervision, and a variety of passing opportunities that arose with the availability of cartoon films, other classes' field trips, and so forth. During the first few weeks, the prices were adjusted to reflect the popularity of the different back-up reinforcers. Lunches and recesses were at an economy cost, and there were no cases after the first two days of children failing to have lunch.

Before we consider the results, it should be pointed out that this was what we sometimes refer to as a "tight" system of contingencies. That is, the circumstances were so arranged that rewards were immediate, and there was *no* way to circumvent the academic responsibilities. Many token systems operate more loosely and often yield results that are less impressive than was the case in this experiment.

The results of the procedures in the experimental classroom were not long in arriving. By the end of the second day the atmosphere had changed almost completely. By that time the class was quiet except for occasional enthusiastic exclamations following successes. The work was being rendered eagerly and rapidly. The change, just in the facial expressions of the children as they approached the teacher, was in sharp contrast to the attitudes that had been described by previous teachers of these children. School, exercise problems, reading, and even the teacher became associated with fun, rewards, success, and a total absence of punitive disciplinary control.

Occasionally an innovative procedure was designed to meet a particular problem. For example, on the first day of classes Chuck had a tantrum. This was no surprise since Chuck's school records indicated frequent tantrums, which usually consisted of falling down and beating his feet and fists against the floor or against nearby walls or furniture. On the occasion of Chuck's first tantrum the teacher had just answered his question, indicating that he could not go to recess without paying a certain number of points, and that points had to be earned by turning in correct exercise sheets. Immediately, as Chuck's tantrum began, the teacher started to tell the class about an ice cream party they could attend with their points at the end of the day and in this manner removed the class's attention from Chuck. Chuck soon looked around, saw that he was getting no attention from the teacher or from the class, and slowly resumed his seat. The teacher then told Chuck quietly that he could have that tantrum free, but more would cost five points each. It was emphasized that he could buy as many as he could afford, but of course that would leave less to spend on other things. That afternoon Chuck had another tantrum, and was asked to pay its cost of five points. There were no more tantrums after that.

Academically, the results of this token economy were highly satisfactory. The children progressed rapidly, without daydreaming or wasting time. In fact, one of the more interesting things was that the children actually seemed annoyed by the types of distractions that they had formerly enjoyed. Early in the program it became obvious that a major challenge was going to be the creation of work fast enough to keep up with the children, who kept gaining on the supply of available exercise sheets. Two extra teachers were brought into the program to help prepare exercise sheets. The set of fourth-grade material, and then a complete set of fifth-grade material were used up by all the students in the class. At the end of the school year, in June of 1969, eight of the ten children had completed the entire set of sixth-grade material and had gone beyond, and one had completed the seventh-grade material. We should again point out that the sets of material made up the entire academic program usually taught at these grade levels, and that the 90-100 percent criterion of mastery is much higher than that usually achieved.

General Principles of the Token Economy

The designer of the token program must adhere to certain principles. Otherwise major problems will surely develop.

1. The student must be capable of performing the expected behavior. It is best to start off at a fairly simple level to insure that everyone is achieving from the first day.
2. Tokens must be given *only* for the occurrence of the proper behavior.
3. The dispensing of tokens must be immediate, to make more visible the behavior-reinforcement contingency.
4. The tokens must be exchangable for items or privileges of value to each student, and the items and privileges should not be attainable outside of token redemption.
5. Reinforcers should be of reasonable magnitude in relation to the amount of effort required to achieve them. Each student must be a frequent "winner." Some, of course, will be bigger winners than others.

6. Punishment should not be employed in the classroom. The five-point "charge" described in the previous example stretched things a bit—as a rule students should never be fined. Time-out rooms are frequently used instead.
7. Ideally the system should begin with a form of continuous reinforcement and later be gradually phased into a system of larger but less frequent payoffs.
8. Back-up reinforcers should be appropriate to the age of the students. Responsibilities, free time, and the like are appropriate to high school programs.

Problems Encountered with Token Economies

Most problems in token programs can be prevented if the principles listed above are carefully followed. Some errors that have ruined token economies include:

1. Punishing a student by taking away his earned tokens. This shatters the continuity of the program and has a bad effect on morale.
2. Leaving the student in class, but preventing him from earning tokens for long intervals of time. This reestablishes the old system in which there were no good reasons for working.
3. Not providing adequate or appropriate back-up reinforcers. This is an obvious opportunity for administrative "economy," but such economy is short-sighted. One should no more expect students to work for trinkets and trash or for nothing than would teachers.
4. Running out of tokens. Even slips of paper stamped with the teacher's name can be prepared for use as temporary tokens.
5. Violating the economy by giving extra tokens preferentially as "bonuses."

Variations on the Token Procedure

Many different methods have been employed in various token programs. For example, rather than actual tokens, large rotary counters operated by the teacher in view of the class have been employed, as have little booklets of punch-cards carried by the students, in which the teacher enters "points."

Back-up reinforcers are variable. Most research has involved material items such as candy, soft drinks, model kits, comic books, snacks, and so forth. The case detailed earlier in this section, in its stress upon nonmaterial privileges, was unusual. Probably a combination of material with nonmaterial reinforcers would be most effective. As long as the school's facilities may be used flexibly, a great many more kinds of nonmaterial reinforcers are possible. A few schools, for example, are beginning to try a system whereby the most skillful children may exchange tokens for short periods of daily "employment" (for a few cents per hour) tutoring the less skillful.

Range of Application

The possible uses of token systems are only beginning to be realized. Thus far the use has been mainly with special groups such as the maladjusted and mentally retarded—groups that are the least successful in ordinary classrooms. However, the technique has been used in a number of ordinary public school classrooms, in ghetto schools, with three- and four-year-old prekindergarten children, and with college students. It has achieved consistently excellent results.

Case

In the university summer session of 1968, the writer taught an introductory psychology class. Of the nineteen students in the class, fourteen had previously failed the course and were repeating it. Such classes do not show typical achievement. Our university's records show that when F students repeat the introductory psychology course, about one-half make another F. Most of the remainder get a grade of D.

The system employed was extremely simple. The text was divided into thirty-one pages per class day. No lectures were used. Instead, each day a list of completion-type questions was prepared. The simpler questions were asked of individual class members in turn. The more difficult ones were asked of the entire group, with the first chance of answering going to the person who first raised his hand. For each correct answer a printed paper token was given. The only explanation of the tokens to the class was that they should be saved. No promise of exchange value was made. The enthusiasm of the class was extremely high, and it was frequently difficult to determine whose hand was raised first. Grades in the course were awarded solely on the basis of four multiple-choice examinations on which previous performance norms were available. Scores required for the various letter grades were the same as had been used the previous fall with the same examinations. On the basis of the multiple-choice examinations, there were 2 A's, 10 B's, 6 C's, and 1 D. There were no F grades in the group. If back-up reinforcers such as periodic applications of token points toward course grades had been provided, the favorable effect on grades probably would have been higher. Still, students will be reinforced by simple pieces of paper, just as they were with gold stars for attendance in Sunday School. It is the factor of being singled out and given something that reinforces. The teacher contemplating this technique should realize, however, that contributions toward the course grade are not particularly effective back-up reinforcers with students below the college level.

Overview

The token economy is deceptively simple. Certain factors are vital for its successful operation. A large number of token economies are made inoperative because of mistakes in design. Others, designed carefully by consultants, have been altered by teachers until they no longer function effectively. Token economies should not be designed or operated without careful adherence to the principles we have discussed in this section.

The token economy is of the most benefit to students who have never been reinforced for achieving since their early efforts were either substandard or were ignored. Whole populations of persons who have never been "winners" may achieve academic success through a token economy. Once they begin to attain reinforcement, they seem not to want to stop. As philosophic observers have pointed out, a privilege withdrawn is more painful than deprivations that have always existed. Meanwhile, they undergo the development of "intrinsic motivation," which is to say they become "self-reinforcers."

The cooperation of school administrators is undoubtedly going to be more easily obtained as they have opportunities to observe the beneficial effects of token programs. Recently, where a new token class was being set up, the principal was asked to allow occasional early dismissal of students as a back-up reinforcer. Students could spend tokens to get out of school at the end of the day, at a rate of so many tokens per fifteen minutes of time. The principal gave his agreement only reluctantly, but later became enthusiastic as he began to see the progress of the class. Getting out of school early became a very popular back-up reinforcer, and students worked exceptionally hard during the usually "lazy" hours of midafternoon in order to buy their freedom. This may seem to be a sort of paradox, but learning was accelerated far beyond its rate prior to the token program.

Two concluding remarks about token economies are in order. First, where such programs have been placed in operation, criticism of "bribery methods" has sometimes been heard. It is an almost invariable fact that the critics do not have children in the program and have no opportunity to directly observe the progress of the students. Second, the token economy, by virtue of the fact that it parallels the "real" economy, teaches students a valuable lesson in life in a relatively painless way. That lesson is that one has to pour forth effort and produce in order to get rewards in life. The token economy does not foster the idea of getting something for nothing.

The token economy is a considerably advanced style of behavior modification, compared with the simple use of praise and attention. It allows a high degree of behavior control. The sophisticated technology may impress some and offend others. A little later in this book we will consider some of the critical remarks made by those who come into contact with token economies and other forms of behavior modification in the schools.

BEHAVIOR MODIFICATION AND THE HIGH SCHOOL STUDENT

9

The reader has undoubtedly been aware that the procedures described so far, despite an example or two taken from college classrooms, seem to have a distinct application to the elementary school classroom. This is partly because the vast preponderance of research and development with normal children has been in elementary schools. Another main reason is that in both elementary schools and institutional settings, where a lot of the research has been done, it is relatively easy for the teacher to control reinforcers. Control of reinforcers is a vital ingredient. When we consider how we might apply behavior modification techniques to older students—those in high schools and, to some extent, junior high schools—we can anticipate a number of problems. A teacher would have to exercise considerable ingenuity to devise workable methods for high-schoolers. Not the least of the problems is the fact that, in our affluent economy, a high school student desiring some tangible item generally has the money to buy it for himself. Outside researchers are no more original in their thinking than anyone else in uncharted territory, and it is probably because of the foreseen difficulties that there is practically no published research on the behavior-modification classroom in the public high school.

Case One

About a year ago we began an experiment in a high school English classroom. It was our intention to apply the methods that we had been developing and using in elementary schools. The classroom teacher had just graduated from the university and knew the basic techniques of behavior modification. She agreed to begin the semester with more-or-less "traditional" methods of classroom instruction. We entered the classroom two weeks into the school term.

After we spent a few days observing the class and they were accustomed to our presence, we began collecting base-rate information on the undesirable types of classroom behavior. There were the usual "misbehaviors"— whispering, talking or laughing, reaching out to touch other students, and so forth. We used a method called *time-sampling*, which in this case consisted of observing one student at a time for a period of fifteen seconds, checking his behavior from a list of misbehaviors, then going to the next student for fifteen seconds, until all of the class had been sampled. In this manner the total class of thirty students was sampled in slightly under eight minutes, after which the sampling cycle could be repeated as often as desired.

The preexperimental base rate showed that approximately 34 percent of the fifteen-second sample periods contained one or more instances of misbehavior. This is a very high rate of misbehavior, but one often sees something of this sort in university laboratory schools at the high school level. We then arranged for the teacher to deliver attention and her approval to desired behaviors and to ignore behaviors that were undesired. The outcome of this practice was dismal. Over a three-week period with this procedure (we called it Phase One) the time-sample showed an increase from a 34 percent base rate of undesirable behavior to a rate of about 38 percent. Such an increase really doesn't create much noticeable change on the surface, but the actual figures told us that the change was there. We decided that the reason for the lack of improvement was that teen-agers have social characteristics different from those in elementary grades. They are, to a large extent, more significantly affected by social reinforcers delivered by their peers and not so much by the adults in their immediate environments.

We then proceeded to Phase Two of the experiment. Here we settled the class into reading and writing exercises. Each student was given mimeographed paragraphs that included errors of spelling and punctuation. His assignment was to rewrite the paragraphs as neatly as possible, correcting as many errors as he could find. Each proper correction on the first attempt was worth two points to the student. After the teacher evaluated the paper and awarded points, she then underlined the entire line where a still uncorrected error occurred and asked the student to recopy the line properly after finding the remaining error. One point was given for each newly corrected error. If necessary, the process was repeated a third time with more specific identification of the exact location of the error. For each one hundred points earned, the student received a coin-like token that, at this stage of the program, could be exchanged at the end of the next grading period for credit toward the letter grade in the course.

During the first full week of this procedure, it appeared that the slowest student was earning about five tokens per week and the most advanced student was earning about fifteen. During the subsequent four weeks, however, we saw the gradual falling-off of earnings, until by the end of the fifth full week of Phrase Two, the slower students were earning around two tokens per week and the class average was down by about two tokens per week from the average rate four weeks earlier. Only the students who were high in token earnings during the first week of Phase Two remained at the initial level.

Before we continue, let us interpret a couple of things that developed during Phase Two. First, it appears that there is an initial reinforcing effect that comes from the introduction of a token economy in the high school. This is a sort of "gold star" effect, by which the awarding of a prize—however meaningless—stimulates performance. Then, when the novelty wears off, interests lag unless the back-up reinforcers are really functioning as reinforcers. Apparently, except for the "good" students, course grades are not very effective back-up reinforcers in the high school.

Also, in all this discussion of tokens in Phase Two, we almost forgot our friends in the right rear corner of the classroom who were time-sampling. But they were there all along and were able to provide us with continuing data on classroom misbehavior. Three things struck us about their data. First, the average percentage of undesirable behaviors in the time-sample blocks of fifteen seconds, which we saw go from a 34 percent base rate to 38 percent in Phase One, dropped to 12 percent in the first week of Phase Two and then gradually increased to 27 percent in the last week of Phase Two. This is still well under the initial base rate. The second finding was extremely interesting. In Phase Two we noticed that the high-token group did *not* go up in the misbehavior rate through the five weeks of Phase Two, as did the average and below-average token groups. Now, for the third and most interesting finding. We looked up the Phase One misbehavior rates and found that our Phase Two high-token, low-misbehavior people had been *no better than average* in their previous Phase One behavior. The implication of this finding is clear. Able students who are just "absorbing" without challenge in the classroom misbehave right along with the other students. It is when they are put to work on a task, with some sort of goal, that they settle down and start working.

We now found ourselves with three more weeks to go before the summer vacation began. Since the English class we were working with met during the last period of the day, we were able to secure approval from the principal to redeem tokens with early release from class on the last day of each week. As we have indicated, the most able students were earning around three tokens a day, with the less able earning approximately one every other day. We decided to let the students buy their release each Friday, with each token earning a five-minute, free-time voucher. The entire fifty-minute class period, then, would cost ten tokens. This procedure was called Phase Three.

The teacher announced the policy on a Monday, and we were hardly prepared for the results. Let us simply say that of the thirty students, only five had to spend *any* time in class on the first Friday, and three of those had been absent during a portion of the week. Even of those five, all but one were able to leave class before the halfway point in the hour. This means that practically the entire class was earning tokens at a rate of around three a day or better, in order to buy the entire hour on Friday. Moreover, the time-sampling procedure showed a drop to an 8 percent rate of misbehavior during the first week of Phase Three, followed by rates of around 5 percent for each of the last two weeks. The number of tokens issued and the number of students completely free on Fridays also stayed about the same the last two weeks. You might remember that this last two weeks was the time just preceding the summer vacation—notoriously unproductive days in most classes.

A colleague who looked over the first draft of this manuscript mentioned the fact that there weren't many cases of failure described, and she knew that failures sometimes occur. Perhaps this is because we customarily rework our procedures after failure, try again, rework again, and so forth before a full-scale program is undertaken. Then when reports are written, we describe our full-scale programs rather than our pilot projects, which are full of errors. The procedures just described in the high school, however, were of a trial-run nature. This is why we fell on our experimental faces when we assumed that teacher attention was a reinforcer for a high-schooler. The writer mentions this to placate his colleague, and he would also like to mention three other surprises that had us worried for a while; the reader may then rest assured that no system is without its problems. The first incident arose when we learned that a certain student was intimidating other token-earners. This student, a large boy who lived in a home for orphans, snatched the tokens of one student in the lunchroom and later on the same day threatened another student with a beating if he did not turn over his tokens to him. This gangster-style extortion effort was luckily nipped in the bud. A second student was discovered trying to trade personal items like a ball-point pen and a deck of playing cards for the tokens of other students. Finally, one ingenious student attempted what might be analogous to counterfeiting. We had arranged to use Mexican five-centavo pieces as tokens because they are easily acquired in quantity quite inexpensively and aren't generally available to students. This student, whose father was a local Spanish teacher, apparently already had a supply and was impulsive enough to try to redeem more than any single student had actually earned during the week. In his case we were able to spot the imbalance between income and expenditure. Such problems and a thousand others—all different—plague behavior-modification programs just as readily as they affect other forms of innovative change, as well as forms of conventional teaching.

Case Two

In our effort to gain control over resources that can be used as back-up reinforcers, we recently hit upon a useful procedure that could be used in certain settings. This experiment has just been completed, and the results are excellent.

The researcher on the scene, who took his first behavior-modification course in the previous summer session of our graduate school, is the director of what is called a "distributive education" program in a large urban high school. This program involves a certain number of students who attend high school classes in the morning and go to jobs at noon. To assure uniformity and relevance in their classroom education, the students are assigned to a packaged curriculum, all attending the same class at the same hour as a group.

In the previous year the employers had paid the student employees on the basis of aspects of the job's difficulty, company affluence, and so forth. Now they were asked to pay the wage earnings directly to the school, with the assurance that every penny would go to the distributive education students. We made the rates of pay contingent upon classroom performance. The students were able to earn points daily in their classes, both through classroom participation and weekly quizzes. At the end of the week the points were added up and the students' rates of pay for the following week were calculated on the point basis. Roughly speaking, the money was in direct proportion to the percentage of the total points earned by all class members. If a student earned less than a bare minimum of points, he worked for the minimum rate of fifty cents per hour for the next week. A very high number of points could result in rates of pay ranging up to $2.85 per hour.

In order to compare performances, we used the same weekly quizzes that had been used in the preceding year. Everything was consistent from the one year to the next—the teachers, the quizzes given every Friday, and even the books used—except for the point-basis for wages. In the preceding year the class had had an average of 64 percent of the questions right on all the quizzes considered together; under the experimental procedure, that percentage was raised to 84 percent. On every quiz the new group was well above the students of the preceding year, and the difference grew increasingly pronounced as the weeks went by. We computed only the data on quiz performance, but the teachers reported many side-effects in the students' behaviors. Never had the classes seemed so "business-like" and the students so serious in their classwork. One teacher reported that he had never really believed that one could get the distributive education students to study until he saw the results of the experiment.

Overview

A real challenge is involved if the teacher is to devise meaningful reinforcers for older students. Since most students at the high school level aren't terribly motivated by either course grades or the teacher's approval, other goals must be devised and used as back-up reinforcers. Free time has been shown to be a powerful reinforcer, but teachers should be prepared to justify its use by rendering evidence that the amount of learning in class with free time made available surpasses the amount without the free-time option. This, again, is why we urge that initial base rates of academic performances or misbehaviors be calculated in behavior-modification classrooms.

GETTING
A PROGRAM
GOING

10

There are a number of important points that might be useful to the teacher who is considering the adoption of behavior-modification techniques in her own classroom.

First, the teacher should figure out what the target behaviors are to be. A *target behavior* is a behavior that one is directly trying to develop. For example, if certain students tease others in the classroom, the target behavior might even be as simple as sitting quietly and reading. Second, a base rate must be established. Failure to do so will obscure any progress. It is not unusual to see disruptive behaviors in a classroom sink to perhaps 30 percent of their original rate and to find the teacher simultaneously depressed because the technique "isn't working."

Once the target behaviors have been specified and base rates charted, then and only then should the reinforcement contingency be initiated. The teacher should not have to wait until the behavior occurs before she can apply reinforcement. Instead, she might suggest proper behavior patterns. In the interest of maintaining classroom variety and interest, it might be best not to specify exactly what sorts of rewards will be delivered. Also, in the same vein, if the teacher specifies the exact contingency relationship, she might find herself committed to a 100 percent schedule of reinforcement that should later be thinned out into a partial schedule.

The next hurdle is one that may tempt the teacher to abandon the program unless she recognizes the problem as it develops. When any behavior is being extinguished—and here we envision the teacher withdrawing attention from undesirable behaviors—those behaviors show a sharp increase in rate for a short period of time. The withdrawal of attention frustrates the child, who then experiences an increased drive state leading to a spurt in the behavior for a period of a few minutes to a few hours.

Following this, there is a falling-off of the behavioral rate, which can be hastened if the teacher can supply reinforcement for proper behavior during this period. If the child in question is not emitting the desired behavior and therefore cannot be reinforced directly, a child seated close by can be the object for reinforcement. This, as we showed earlier, can actually reinforce the observing child to an extent, the process being known as vicarious reinforcement.

When the child who is the momentary object of the teacher's effort finally begins to respond to the program, he should not be left dangling—at this point he is extremely vulnerable to rapid extinction. He should gain as much continuous reinforcement as the teacher is able to provide. Gradually, as reinforcements accumulate, the variability of the "good" behaviors decreases and they become more habitual in that their rates rise swiftly.

The teacher must be careful to do her best to treat all children equally —that is, no child should have many of his desirable behaviors ignored for a considerable period of time because the teacher is spending her time reinforcing the behaviors of only one or two particular students. Otherwise the children may switch many of their strategies, and the teacher may begin to see what seems like a personality change in some children as they investigate other means of gaining attention within the framework of the behavior-modification classroom. One of the most common developments is the creation of the dependent personality. Some children who function well may begin to need "help" from the teacher. This is particularly true in classrooms where individualized instruction materials are being used. It is important for the teacher to learn whether the help is really needed. In order to find this out, it is sometimes helpful to go to a system in which the student who finishes first with a perfect paper is given a few extra points to work as a tutor, thus relieving the teacher of this function. If the help requested by the newly "dependent" student is simply a bid for adult attention, such requests stop at this point.

The teacher must continue to chart behaviors to the degree that she can do so efficiently, even if the charting is limited to rates gathered on only one or two specific students.

Reinforcers to back up tokens or classroom points must occupy the continued thinking of the teacher, day by day. There should be change and variety in the entire situation, just as there should be in a regular classroom, in order to maintain the attention and the continued interest of the students. Since the back-up reinforcers are so vital, they should be as varied as circumstances allow. Even with the so-called "reinforcement menu" used at some schools, where students can examine an entire list of rewards and associated costs in points, the same repetitious rewards pale after a time. The teacher might even enlist the support of the children to get more ideas about what sorts of back-up reinforcers would be appealing.

What To Do with Limited Resources

Severe limitations may be placed on the teacher by administrators unfamiliar with the value of reinforcement principles. While in some ghetto programs entire classrooms of poor students have earned tokens during the first half hour of school, with which to buy breakfast in the school cafeteria, there are those who criticize such a program for "dangling food before a hungry child." While 100 percent of the children in such programs get breakfast instead of the previous small percentage who were lucky enough to be fed before the program's origin, there are persons who will object to any form of food reinforcement. (This is peculiar in a historically agriculture-based country where chores-before-breakfast was a common rule.) The intelligent teacher, however, can devise many interesting alternatives to material means of reinforcement.

1. She might post pictures of children—the prize winners of the day—on a bulletin board. This has proven to be a very effective back-up reinforcer for elementary-age children.
2. She might let winners amuse others in the classroom by doing skits or other performances.
3. She should be aware of the "Premack principle." Premack discovered that *any* naturally high-rate behavior can be used to reinforce low-rate behaviors. High-rate behaviors are obviously popular and rewarding to the individuals who emit them, so their permission can be made contingent upon the occurrence of any low-rate behaviors that the teacher may consider valuable.

The Problem of Large Classes

Critics of behavior modification frequently point to the fact that the examples usually cited involve considerable classroom attention—a luxury not permitted in the large classroom. They ask if one can apply these practices with a large group. Of course there should not be classes of thirty or forty children. However, in view of the often unavoidable necessity for large classes, we feel the proper attitude is that there is no "class" as an entity—only a collection of individuals. Probably most teachers now spend a considerable amount of their day interacting with certain individuals rather than with the class as a whole. At the very least we may take the interactions that already exist and give them the flavor of behavior modification. That is, attention should be given to performance and achievement of both a social and an academic nature, and attention should be taken away from undesirable actions. Furthermore, because of the phenomenon called vicarious reinforcement, which has been previously mentioned, rates of certain behaviors of the observing children go up when they see those behaviors reinforced in another individual. So the criticism, at least if taken from the frame of reference of the regular classroom, has little merit.

Also, the teacher should remember, if she hesitates to use behavior-modification techniques because of class size, that she might go into it gradually. Just the employment of social reinforcers with a handful of the children in her classroom may be enough to give her the confidence to go ahead with her other ideas for reinforcement. Elaborate things should follow simple beginnings.

Developing and Keeping Up with Techniques

In order to keep abreast of the vital literature and learn about further procedures, the teacher should be prepared to examine sources of additional information. By now she should be so expert in handling the vocabulary of the field as to have little or no difficulty in reading from a variety of technical sources. In this section we list further sources, and the teacher should be on the alert for newer ones that will continue to appear on the market. The following list is not represented to be at all complete. Rather, these are some of the sources that seem quite appealing and may be of most interest to teachers. Furthermore, the teacher may find it helpful, after becoming familiar with some of the sources, to refer interested parents to them for information about use in the home setting.

General Texts

There are certain books that go into behavior theory itself in detail even though they do not directly treat the topic of classroom procedures. These five are listed below in an estimated order of increasing difficulty.

Keller, F. S. *Learning: Reinforcement theory.* New York: Random House, 1969.
Reynolds, G. S. *A primer of operant conditioning.* Glenview, Ill.: Scott, Foresman, 1968.
Wenrich, W. W. *A primer of behavior modification.* Belmont, Calif.: Brooks-Cole, 1970.
Lundin, R. W. *Personality: A behavioral analysis.* New York: Macmillan, 1969.
Millenson, J. R. *Principles of behavioral analysis.* New York: Macmillan, 1967.

General Readings (Edited)

Ullman, L. P., & Krasner, L. (Eds.) *Case studies in behavior modification*. New York: Holt, Rinehart and Winston, 1965.
Ulrich, R., Stachnik, T., & Mabry, J. (Eds.) *Control of human behavior*, Vol. I. Glenview, Ill.: Scott, Foresman, 1966.
Ulrich, R., Stachnik, T., & Mabry, J. (Eds.) *Control of human behavior*, Vol. II. Glenview, Ill.: Scott, Foresman, 1970.

Classroom Applications

Madsen, C. H., Jr., & Madsen, C. K. *Teaching / dicipline: Behavioral principles toward a positive approach*. Boston: Allyn and Bacon, 1970.
Meacham, M. L., & Wiesen, A. E. *Changing classroom behavior: A manual for precision teaching*. Scranton, Pa.: International Textbook, 1969.
O'Leary, K. L., & O'Leary, S. G. *Classroom management: The successful use of behavior modification*. New York: Pergamon, in press.
Sulzer, B., & Mayer, G. R. *Behavior modification procedures for school personnel*. Hinsdale, Ill.: Dryden Press, in press.

Classroom Applications—Readings

Benson, F. A. (Ed.) *Modifying deviant school behaviors in various classroom settings*. Eugene, Ore.: University of Oregon Department of Special Education, 1969.
Fargo, G. A., Behrns, C., & Nolen, P. A. (Eds.) *Behavior modification in the classroom*. Belmont, Calif.: Wadsworth, 1970.
Haring, N., & Whelan, R. (Eds.) *The learning environment: Relation to behavior modification and implications for special education*. Lawrence, Kans.: University of Kansas Press, 1966.
Rubadean, D. O., & Hertzman, A. J. (Eds.) *Behavior modification techniques for the classroom*. Waltham, Mass.: Ginn-Blaisdell, in press.

Additional Background Interest

Browning, R. M., & Stover, D. O. *Behavior modification in child treatment*. Chicago: Aldine, in press.
Skinner, B. F. *The technology of teaching*. New York: Appleton, 1968.
Valett, R. E. *Modifying children's behavior: A guide for parents and professionals*. Palo Alto, Calif.: Fearon Publishers, 1969.

ARGUMENTS
AND QUESTIONS
ABOUT BEHAVIOR
MODIFICATION

It seems that there a number of things left unsaid, and many will remain so, about the new field of behavior modification. So far we have not touched significantly upon the challenges to behavior modification put by many of its critics. We cannot pretend that the techniques of behavior modification are completely above criticism and improvement. However, they do appear to be highly effective in meeting what are typically urgent needs. Be that as it may, let us examine a few of the remarks made by critics of behavior modification and reply to them.

"Behavior Is Complex"

On the one hand, some critics of behavior modification have stated that we tend to oversimplify human nature, and of course they are right to a degree. Probably every attempt to understand man's behavior fails to recognize certain vital aspects of the human function. On the other hand, behavior modification does recognize that any single aspect of behavior is made up of a complex array of basic factors. For example, through research we have combined conditioning and extinction procedures in such a way as to verify that what we refer to as "racial prejudice" is actually a combination of several behaviors with somewhat independent causes. These behaviors, or psychological experiences, are (1) classically conditioned emotional orientations, (2) operantly reinforced opinions, (3) operantly reinforced verbal habits of "labelling" people, and (4) to a certain degree, rationally arrived-at conclusions. Such a viewpoint hardly seems like oversimplification when compared with the simplistic notions about racial prejudice maintained by many people—even some experts.

Similarly, while we recognize the important contribution of the respondent basis for aggression in the frustrations of the environment and inescapable punishments, we also know of research that shows how swiftly the rate of aggression will rise when it leads to positive or negative operant reinforcement. Thus aggression as well as prejudice, ambition, religiosity, affections, aversions, and a host of other behaviors and experiences of human beings are recognized as being simple only in that we try to isolate the antecedent factors and study their effects on the behavior in question. This simple-appearing approach, then, which constitutes the basic scientific method, has made it possible for us to achieve an influence over behavior to a degree unheard of with philosophic approaches.

"Lack of Warmth"

When only the most superficial impressions of the behavior-modification approach have been gained, an immediate criticism often heard is that the proponents of behavior modification seem to be insensitive to human feelings. Critics infer a lack of warmth and feeling, perhaps drawn from terminology such as "reinforcement" rather than "love," "levels of psychological experience" rather than "the whole child," and so forth. Actually there is a great deal of human warmth in behavior-modification classrooms. Reinforcers are given by human beings, accompanied by genuine praise and affection. Many behavior-modification-oriented teachers were first attracted to the approach as much by the kindness and better emotional interactions it offered as alternatives to punishment as they were by its demonstrated effectiveness. A frequent reaction of teachers to their early experiences in a behavior-modification program, moreover, is that, under the praise and reward conditions, they actually find themselves actively searching for the good in each and every child. This has a great effect upon the entire way in which the teacher perceives the basic motives of others. The rewards that follow—the smiles, pats on the shoulder, and praise—are then just as sincere as is the basic nature of the teacher generating them.

"People Are Treated like Machines"

A similar criticism of behavior modification reflects the critic's feeling that the whole philosophy behind the approach is mechanistic—the human being is seen as reacting in an unfeeling manner and is essentially "depersonalized." The argument here is a basic one. In the physical sciences the deterministic viewpoint is that which assumes that there are consistent cause-and-effect relationships behind all physical events. The deterministic viewpoint has proven effective in the biological sciences as well, to the extent that it now appears inconceivable to view either normal or pathological processes of the human body in any other way. More recently the deterministic viewpoint was applied to behavior. Causes are assumed to exist for all behaviors, and none are assumed to have just happened spontaneously without a reason. The search for the "reasons" in this framework has paid dividends in assisting psychologists to understand the complex patterns even of mental patients whose bizarre acts otherwise defy analysis. A reinforcement-oriented determinism assumes that behavior—normal or pathological—occurs because the individual gets something out of it.

Many human beings, however, do not appreciate the view that their behavior is not subject to their own "free will." Despite evidence that one is largely a product of his reinforcement history, many people still like to think that they can alter their actions and their attitudes at a moment's notice by simply deciding to do so. If that were true, we could handle many agonizing problems involving jealousy, social timidity, sexual conflicts, anxieties regarding aging and death, and the like by simply approaching the problem rationally and "understanding" it. Such is not the case, however, and it is interesting that the same persons who insist that their own behavior is a product of their rational free will are among the first to believe that the behavior of *others* is determined by environmental influence. For example, many feel that the actions of children and youth are strongly influenced by the types of homes in which they develop, the quality of their companions, the sorts of motion pictures they view, and an array of other presumed influences. At least the behavior-modification advocates agree with such critics on the general point that the environment can have a strong influence on behavior. We may even agree with the critics on some of their favorite popular beliefs about causes. Among other factors, for example, research has shown that the interactions of a child with his parents and peers has a strong influence, in terms of both the consequences of his styles of interaction and the imitative models provided him by others; and, in general, the entire pattern of success (reinforcement) and failure (extinction or punishment) early in life has a lingering influence on the child's life style.

The criticisms of the deterministic viewpoint often center around the use of words like "mechanical" or statements that desired patterns can be "programmed" through reinforcement. Let us take this opportunity to point out that such expressions are used in an analogous sense for their descriptive value. We certainly recognize the human complexities and the need for a total approach to child development. The expressions that seem to suggest that we seek to develop mechanically acting automatons actually translate to reflect every parent and teacher's intention for children to show well-developed patterns of proper social behavior, work habits, academic skills, and social attitudes.

The Ethics of Behavioral Control

Many persons are strongly aware of the implications, for society, of programs for the control of human behavior. Obviously the power of behavioral control can be welcomed for the good that it can do or feared for its possible misuse. The results depend largely on the motives of those in key positions. In a democratic society there is less to fear from innovative programs than in other societies, and the Americans' level of awareness of public practices also offers protection. There are, however, some basic considerations that must accompany any claim that man's freedom is lessened by deliberate programs of environmental design. Following is a rationale of deterministic psychology in a logical progression:

1. The behavior of a typical individual in society is in no way "free." It is determined to a marked degree by the nature of the circumstances that contribute to his drive state and by the environmental factors that provide the occasions for both rewarding and aversive experiences.
2. At present these environmental factors are left largely to chance or to human whim, with uneven results. Those in fortunate circumstances emerge as "winners"—successful and effective citizens—while those with less favorable backgrounds eventually experience frustration and various degrees of failure.
3. The behavior modifier simply attempts to arrange the environment in such a way as to maximize the development of productive behavior habits so that each individual may come closer to achieving his full potential.

In view of the points just stated, we must ask the question, Is the adult who is practicing habits of diligence and industry any less free than another person who is controlled by habits of work-avoidance or resentfulness of work assignments? The answer is obvious. The first mentioned individual is no less free. In fact, his early training has placed him in a position of being more free to control the available reinforcers in his society. A recent popular song defined freedom as "nothing left to lose," and, in large measure, proper environmental design should keep many persons from this sort of eventuality.

The goals of behavior modification are no different from the goals of general education. Those goals are to produce individuals who are effective in their work and in their social interactions and reasonably fitted to meaningful participation in the social and political institutions of the nation. Patterns of disruption, aggression, and inactivity have disastrous effects on the adult who employs them, and it is a cruel hoax to allow such patterns to develop unchecked in the children and youth of our schools.

Carry-Over into Other Situations

In certain cases, improvements produced in the behavior-modification classroom carry over (generalize) into other situations. Only a few studies have reported the recurrence of old patterns in children returning to regular classrooms after a term in a behavior-modification setting. So far the findings have been that the children continue to manifest the improved behaviors, but their long-term continuance is up to the teacher, who must be perceptive to the improvements and give them social reinforcement. Otherwise the behaviors will extinguish, and the child will return to the patterns that were effective in procuring reinforcement prior to the behavior modification. In most situations the child should have a new advantage —he has work habits and skills that he never previously possessed.

Occasionally parents wonder if the child will not come to expect rewards and if this will produce problems. Certainly the child will develop an expectation that people are taking an interest in his performance and that when he achieves they will express their approval of his success. If this is unrealistic, it is only because many teachers and parents have less time to give to their charges than do most employers later in the individual's professional life. Even if the child does grow disappointed at being ignored, there have been no reports of depression or extreme negativism after a child has returned from a behavior-modification program to a regular classroom.

The topic of possible generalization of the improved behavior to the home has been treated in a number of journal articles. After a few days or a few weeks in the behavior-modification program, children usually show greater cooperativeness in the home and less resistance to rules and requests. There have even been reports of parents noting an increase in the number of affectionate overtures from the child—possibly because the child is happier. To prevent the possibility of eventual discriminative conditioning, which might result in one pattern of behavior in the school and another in the home, the teacher might consider encouraging the parents to follow a few parallel procedures on their own. Parents could be shown appropriate ways of reinforcing improved social patterns, completion of difficult chores, and completion of homework assignments without significant errors.

Talking with Parents and Teachers

Parents seldom admit to being expert at matters of educational procedure, with only a few usually dismaying exceptions. Many express interest and may ask questions that go beyond the simple technology of the approach. Probably a behavior-modification-oriented teacher receives as many questions from other teachers as from parents. Most teachers are concerned about educational issues and are genuinely interested in the innovations being tried by other teachers. Only occasionally does one run up against a teacher who is so adamantly against behavior modification as to be unreached by logic or evidence.

Teachers may be interested to learn that behavior modification is based on the principles of learning. Of all people, teachers are in the best position to appreciate both the complexity and the significance of the learning process. It is also relevant that, in a sense, the deliberate change of behavior patterns—hence, behavior modification—is the literal definition of the teacher's role in the classroom. If she is hired to modify behavior, then an understanding of the field of behavior modification would seem appropriate.

As we draw to a conclusion, we would like to present to you some short interchanges that have taken place from time to time as we have travelled about and presented the topic of behavior modification to various parents and educators.

Q   In these programs do you ever get the feeling that the children are so tense about getting the rewards that they become upset or nervous?

A   We have never seen any evidence of this. We do know that fear of punishment has a very upsetting effect, but the motive structure that is oriented toward rewards seldom brings this emotional condition unless the reward is displayed and the child is deliberately blocked from achieving it. That sort of frustration should never occur in a behavior-modification class.

Q   How do you know that the children are happier with such programs? You say they smile a lot and seem more cheerful, but is there any other proof of this?

A   One of the most interesting pieces of data coming out of our project in the laboratory school, described in Chapter Eight, was the attendance record. The children went from a lower-than-average attendance record to an above-average one in just a few days, and this change was maintained throughout the program. Where before a child might complain of a stomach ache and stay home, I would presume he now endures a minor ache so as to get to school and earn some points.

Q   Isn't such a system bribery?

A   Bribery is a loaded word. Let me take a moment and show you how we are all bribed constantly. We bribe a dog with dog biscuits to learn a trick. We bribe someone to mow our lawn by offering a couple of dollars for the job. We ourselves even get bribed—both you and I are bribed to work by means of our paychecks.

Q   Yes, but that isn't what I mean. You talk of employment, but I am talking about a person who ought to want to learn because it is the right thing to do, without mixing in mercenary values.

A   You have said two things that I will mention. First, you have said it's the "right thing to do." I would submit that teaching is a "right thing," because it is of inestimable benefit to students. Yet, how many teachers would keep on doing this "right thing" if their reinforcers were cut off? Second, you used the phrase "ought to want to." The statement, "you really ought to want to," is so familiar and so admitting of complete defeat, and it completely characterizes the feeble motivating forces that many persons attempt to employ in motivating children. Somehow I doubt that this answer will completely convince you, but perhaps the fact that behavior modification *works* will carry some weight on this issue.

Q   Don't children who always receive rewards get spoiled?

A   I wonder if you really mean "spoiled"? I'll tell you what I think the word means. I think a spoiled child is one who gets everything he wants without having to put out any effort. That is where I would draw an important line—I give you things and you become spoiled, but you earn them and it is an entirely different story. What would you think of a college-age boy who, as soon as he came to the college town, went out and got a job so as to supplement his expense money and be able to purchase the things he needs? Most such boys are accustomed to "rewards" in the sense that their honest efforts in the past have been rewarded with wages, and they are quite self-reliant. That isn't the same as being spoiled.

Q   I don't know if I would want to be in a place where I couldn't do things with the other people there unless I had earned points. I think this would take away my dignity.

A   Who has the most dignity—the underachiever and failure or the same child who can gain the dignity that comes with beginning to have success and the respect of others? I will concede your point to the extent that there are some children who have minimal need for such an environment. The bright children who have always been encouraged by their parents already may have dignity in the classroom. But even they don't object to the behavior-modification setup. Like the other kids, they seem to enjoy it.

Q   What is your general feeling about group rewards?

A   Let me make two questions out of your one. First, what do I think of rewarding a group on the basis of the group's collective effort? In general,

I have no particular objection. I must say that it is difficult to tighten up group contingencies to the extent that a given child can't loaf along and let others do the work and then take a portion of the credit and the reward for himself. This is a motivating system that is excellent with four out of five children, but the fifth one needs to be more directly challenged through a system of individual contingencies. I will make a second question now, based on yours. What do I think of withholding the reward from everyone until every single child comes up to some standard? This, I would say, is an entirely different question. I recently discussed this with a few school psychologists who were convinced that the "pressure" that other students would put on the slow or the deviant individuals would assist the progress of the class as a whole. I must say this seems to me to be a slightly unethical practice, very similar to punishing a whole class for the misbehavior of one student. The end result is that the offender gets beaten up or rejected socially by the others, and this seems unfair to me. I must confess that this is just my own opinion, but I don't encourage this type of group reward process.

Q   I heard you speak of "controlling" human behavior, and I think this can get a little frightening. I wonder if the values and objectives of behavior modification are my own. Suppose I don't want my child to be a certain way, and yet the behavior modification people want to turn him into that very thing?

A   This is an excellent question, and first I want to make absolutely clear that techniques and objectives are entirely separate and should not be confused. The techniques are ways to develop behavior rapidly. The objectives are anything you want them to be. I have heard the question phrased, "Who controls the controller?" There are two answers. First, let's agree that the teachers now do their best to change behavior into what they believe are socially desirable patterns. If we can agree on this, we simply are now growing afraid because it appears that the teacher can be more effective in her job. So, in the long run it boils down to a second question— Do we trust our teachers? I would certainly think that there is such a thing as a "socially accepted" pattern of behavior—honesty, industriousness, and the like, which is not really questionable. The teacher has no responsibility to clear these values with parents or administrators before attempting to instill them in her classroom charges. On the other hand, I think that most teachers, when faced with an unusual problem—one that seems questionable in any way—sit down with parents and come to a mutually satisfactory decision as to objectives. If this is done, then the parents have no reason to fear the control capabilities that are within the grasp of teachers.

Q   I have a question about the long-range use of candy, comic books, and so forth for your "back-up" reinforcers. Do you actually advocate such a system of prizes year after year?

A   No. The most important goal of the teacher, in using a token economy, is to create a sensitivity to contingencies. That is, she is trying, in the
long run, to wean the students away from "artificial" reinforcers. First the
students go from having each proper behavior reinforced to waiting for
longer-term rewards, then to a greater appreciation of teacher-approval,
and finally to a "self-reinforcing" condition in which they, themselves,
deliver self-approval for proper behaviors, thereby reinforcing themselves
through their own satisfaction.

Q   I have taught a class and have allowed the better students to go to
the back of the room and read some interesting paperback books as their
reward for doing good work. I think this is the same as what you are
advocating.

A   Yes it is. You have found an effective reinforcer. The only qualifica-
tion I would put upon calling this a simple behavior-modification program
is to ask whether all children, eventually, finish the lesson at the criterion
level and are then reinforced. Usually in situations of the kind you
describe only a handful of children are winners, day after day. This not
only has no reinforcing effect on the nonwinners, but actually can have
a detrimental effect through frustration.

Q   You have mentioned how punishment calls attention to a child
and may actually strengthen the behavior being punished. I think I see
how this works, but I wonder if you can't give some kind of penalties
without a lot of individual attention and somehow keep using a penalty
system in the classroom.

A   Obviously teachers like to use punishment. Every time they use it,
they are reinforced by the temporary lull in misbehavior. You have an
excellent idea in making punishment "attentionless," but this is somewhat
harder to do than you perhaps realize. If you think you can do so, try it,
but let me tell you of an experience that occurred recently. A teacher used
red and green lapel cards with eleven-year-olds in an EMH (Educable
Mentally Handicapped) classroom. Good behavior earned a green-card
punch and bad behavior got a red-card punch. When the green card was
punched, the teacher made remarks about how good the performance
was, while the red card was punched in absolute silence. At the end of the
day, the children had pieces of candy counted out to them equal to the
number of punches in the green card. Then the number of pieces equal to
the number of red punches was taken back and the children kept the
remainder. We found that the children under the red-and-green system
misbehaved *more* than they did under a system of just a green card used
alone. In short, I don't think we actually should keep on punishing, thinking that we can't do without this form of control.

Q   This approach really is dropping the teacher down to a giver-of-
reinforcers, isn't it?

A   Well, I could question the use of the word "down." Maybe this is the highest purpose—a function that can't be taken over by any teaching machine or anyone other than a warm, communicating human being. Anyway, I wish to point out that the system we have been discussing is a *motivating* system—not a teaching system. When a teacher shows children how to perform math calculations or how to differentiate adverbs from adjectives, she has to be excellent at getting to the rational thought processes of the children. Behavior modification doesn't take anything away from this role.

In Conclusion

Various social factors have combined to make teaching in today's schools particularly difficult. Teachers need techniques that work. Many approaches to education ride on the glibness of a theory or do not lend themselves to actual testing. Behavior modification, on the other hand, is being exhaustively researched. According to every test to which they have been put, these techniques work.

The teacher who attempts to shift her style of teaching and motivating children usually has a difficult time making the transition. We hope that she will keep at it long enough to see the powerful effects that the proper use of behavior-modification techniques can produce. Soon she will find herself acting automatically, and when a child does not behave as desired, she will be able to place herself in his position and ask, "Why should I?" Behavior modification, then, can provide the reasons.

GLOSSARY
OF TERMS

BACK-UP REINFORCERS   In token exchange systems, the material items or privileges that are gained in exchange for points or tokens.

BASE RATE   The rate of a given behavior, measured before any experimental treatment. The object is the eventual comparison of the base rate with post-treatment rates.

BEHAVIOR DEFICIT   Failure by a subject to emit specific social, academic, or vocational behaviors at a rate appropriate for his age group.

BEHAVIOR EXCESS   The emitting of behaviors by a subject that either are inherently undesirable, such as classroom disruption, or are rendered undesirable by their high rates, such as excessive dependency actions.

BEHAVIOR MODIFICATION   The manipulation of behavior rates through the application of the principles of the experimental analysis of behavior. The procedures involve the control of environmental variables, in contrast to approaches that stress a subject's "insight," "self-awareness," and the like.

BEHAVIOR THEORY   A comprehensive approach to the behavior of organisms that stresses, as a unified whole, the various principles established through the experimental analysis of behavior.

BEHAVIOR THERAPY   The branch of behavior modification that deals with the sorts of behaviors that may lead to institutionalization, to referral to specialists by parents, or to self-referral—that is, the so-called "clinical" cases.

CHAINING   The linking, in sequence, of various operant acts into a behavioral unit. Each behavioral element yields stimulus elements triggering the next behavioral element, and the final behavioral element gains immediate reinforcement.

CLASSICAL CONDITIONING   The association, through learning, of two stimuli. One, the unconditioned stimulus, is a biologically relevant stimulus in that it reflexively, and without prior training, elicits a particular response. Classical conditoning then occurs when a previously neutral stimulus (the conditioned stimulus), through being paired with the unconditioned stimulus, acquires the ability to elicit the same response.

CONDITIONED REINFORCER   A stimulus that has acquired reinforcing characteristics after having been initially neutral. Conditioned reinforcers are developed as conditioned stimuli within the context of classical conditioning.

CONDITIONED RESPONSE (CR)   In classical conditioning, the response that occurs to the conditioned stimulus after a sufficient number of CS–UCS pairings.

CONDITIONED STIMULUS (CS)   In classical conditioning, the initially neutral stimulus that is repeatedly paired with a biologically relevant stimulus (the UCS).

CONDITIONING   Simple association learning, usually (but not necessarily) nonverbal in nature. There are two forms of conditioning, classical conditioning and operant conditioning.

CONTINGENCY RELATIONSHIP (ALSO CONTINGENT)   A relationship in which a stimulus, whether reinforcer or punisher, is said to be contingent (dependent) upon a behavior; that is, the occurrence of the behavior produces the stimulus and the absence of the behavior causes the absence of the stimulus.

CONTINUOUS REINFORCEMENT   The reinforcement of all (100 percent) or virtually all behaviors of a given class. Continuous reinforcement is contrasted with *Partial Reinforcement*. See also *Reinforcement*.

DEFICIT   See *Behavior Deficit*.

DIFFERENTIAL REINFORCEMENT   A procedure that increases the rate of a specific behavior from among several that are typically emitted in a given situation. The target behavior is reinforced, while reinforcement is carefully withheld from the other behaviors, until the target behavior becomes the dominant pattern.

DISCRIMINATIVE CONDITIONING   The procedure of bringing an operant behavior under stimulus control. By reinforcing the behavior in the presence of a given stimulus (the discriminative stimulus) but not in its absence, the stimulus acquires the capacity to control the operant behavior through its presence or absence.

ELICITED BEHAVIOR   A response involuntarily drawn from an organism, as contrasted with emitted behavior. Reflexive responses designated as UCRs and CRs are elicited by their stimuli.

EMITTED BEHAVIOR   A behavior occurring voluntarily. *Operant Behavior* is emitted.

EXPERIMENTAL ANALYSIS OF BEHAVIOR   The application of known laboratory principles, primarily from the fields of conditioning, learning, and perception, to the prediction and control of the behaviors of organisms.

EXTINCTION   The reduction in rate and perhaps eventual elimination of a behavior. In operant conditioning, extinction involves the nonreinforcement of the behavior whenever it occurs. In classical conditioning, extinction involves the presentation of the CS without pairing with a UCS.

FADING (OR "PROMPTING AND FADING")   A procedure in which an individual is given questions on incompletely learned material, along with cues or partial answers (prompts). He then experiences the same questions with gradual removal of the prompts.

HIGHER-ORDER CONDITIONING A situation following initial classical conditioning in which the CS in the initial conditioning is used as if it were a UCS, paired with a new CS. The new CS may, eventually, elicit some measure of the same response as did the initial UCS, even though those two stimuli have never been paired.

INCOMPATIBLE BEHAVIOR Behaviors that cannot be emitted (or elicited) simultaneously.

MOTOR LEARNING The learning of physical movements.

NEGATIVE REINFORCEMENT The procedure whereby the rate of an operant behavior increases because that behavior lessens or eliminates an aversive stimulus.

NEUTRAL STIMULUS A stimulus that does not elicit responses other than attention when it is presented to a subject.

OPERANT BEHAVIOR (SOMETIMES CALLED AN OPERANT) A type of behavior that is emitted by an individual, is usually visible to others, and that produces some effect on the environment or on the behaving individual's relation to the environment.

OPERANT CONDITIONING The process considered to underlie the increase in those behaviors that immediately precede a reinforcing stimulus. See *Positive Reinforcement; Negative Reinforcement*.

PARTIAL REINFORCEMENT The process by which a percentage of occurrences of a given behavior, noticeably more than 0 percent and noticeably less than 100 percent, gain reinforcement. This is in contrast to *Continuous Reinforcement*. All other things being equal, partial reinforcement gives a behavior greater resistance to extinction than does continuous reinforcement, this phenomenon being known as the partial-reinforcement effect.

POSITIVE REINFORCEMENT The procedure whereby the rate of an operant behavior increases because that behavior acquires some pleasant or appetitive stimulus.

PREMACK PRINCIPLE The discovery that a low-rate behavior can be reinforced by following it with permission or the opportunity to perform behaviors that occur naturally at a high rate. Thus, reinforcers can be taken from the natural environment and need not necessarily be artificially contrived.

PRIMARY REINFORCER A biologically relevant stimulus that can serve to reinforce behavior without the necessity of prior training.

PROMPTING See *Fading*.

PUNISHMENT The presentation of an aversive stimulus following some operant behavior. The effect is suppression of the operant rate. Punishment is defined here as involving stimulus delivery, in contrast to *Time-Out* procedures.

REINFORCEMENT The phenomenon of an operant-rate increase when operant behavior is followed by goal acquisition.

REINFORCER A stimulus that increases the rate of an operant behavior that it immediately follows. See *Positive Reinforcement, Negative Reinforcement*.

RESPONDENT BEHAVIOR A response that is elicited by a stimulus.

RESPONDENT CONDITIONING See *Classical Conditioning*.

RESPONSE An individual element of behavior.

SECONDARY REINFORCER   See *Conditioned Reinforcer.*

SELF-REINFORCEMENT   A hypothetical situation in which mental processes such as insight into a problem's solution, awareness of being correct, the experience of completing a difficult task, and so forth, become conditioned reinforcers and thereafter sustain certain classes of behavior.

SHAPING   The process by which reinforcement is differentially applied to those responses that constitute a closer and closer approximation to the final form of behavior that is desired.

SOCIAL REINFORCER   A reinforcing stimulus that consists of a social interaction. Social reinforcers are attention, affection, approval, and the submission of others. Social reinforcers are contrasted with material reinforcers or privileges.

STIMULUS GENERALIZATION   A conditioned response to a stimulus that is similar but not identical to a previously developed conditioned stimulus.

SUPPRESSION   A reduction in the rate of an operant behavior due to punishment.

TARGET BEHAVIOR   The behavior that is selected for differential reinforcement. Alternatively, in extinction programs, the behavior selected for deliberate nonreinforcement.

TIME-OUT   A procedure used as an alternative to punishment. The individual is removed for a short time from the situation in which others are earning tokens or otherwise gaining positive reinforcement. Thus, time-out involves stimulus removal in contrast to punishment's stimulus delivery.

TIME SAMPLING   A procedure for measuring behavior rates that contrasts with the total count of behaviors occurring in a group. In time sampling, each child is individually observed for a short length of time, and a notation is made as to the occurrence or nonoccurrence of the target behavior. Attention then shifts to the next child, and so on. Time sampling is usually employed in measurement of large groups.

TOKEN   An item having no value in itself, such as a plastic coin, that is given as a reward and can be redeemed in a token-exchange program for items or privileges that are of value.

TOKEN ECONOMY   A token-exchange program in which every privilege, luxury, and necessity must be bought with earned tokens.

TOKEN-EXCHANGE PROGRAM   A situation in which the subject can earn tokens by emitting certain behaviors. The tokens can then be exchanged for other rewards such as privileges or material items.

UNCONDITIONED RESPONSE (UCR)   In classical conditioning, the response that is elicited by the *Unconditioned Stimulus.*

UNCONDITIONED STIMULUS (UCS)   In classical conditioning, the stimulus that is biologically relevant in that it "naturally" elicits some measurable response from the subject without prior training.

VICARIOUS REINFORCEMENT   An increase in the rate of a subject's target behavior that follows his observing another individual being reinforced for that behavior.

INDEX

I

Ignoring (*see* Attention)
Imitative behavior, 34
Immaturity, 37
Incompatible behaviors, 33
Intrinsic motivation, 26–27, 60
Isolation, 36

L

Large classes, 70–71
Limited resources, 70

M

Mental blocks, 7, 17
Mentally retarded youngsters, 41
Money as reinforcer, 66

O

Operant behavior, 5
  sources of, 33
Operant conditioning, 19–28, 40–46
  extinction of, 31, 68
  simultaneous classical conditioning, 27, 42, 73
Orientations (*see* Emotional orientations)

P

Premack principle, 70
Prompting and fading, 45
Punishment, 47–51, 81

R

Racial prejudice, 35, 73–74
Random behaviors, 33–34
Rational behavior, 5–8
Reading, 17
  on behavior-modification topics, 71–72

Reinforcers, 19
Reinforcement, 20–28, 40
  conditioned, 24
  differential, 45–46
  immediacy of, 40
  negative, 42
  positive, 42
  primary, 20–24
  schedules of, 40–41, 68
  social, 24–25
  vicarious, 34
Released time as reinforcer, 60, 65
Respondent behavior, 4, 9–10

S

Scientific determinism, 3, 74–75
Self-reinforcement (*see* Intrinsic motivation)
Sensitivity to contingencies, 52, 81
Shaping, 43, 44
Speech, 15–16, 19, 35
Spelling, 31–32, 43
Spoiled children, 79
Stimulus, conditioned, 10
  unconditioned, 10
Stimulus generalization, 14–16
Students as tutors, 59
Subject matter, enjoyment of, 18
Submission of others, 25
Suppression, 48

T

Target behaviors, 67
Tension in students, 78
Time-out procedures, 50–51
Time sampling, 63
Token economies, 52–61
  principles of, 57
  problems in, 58

V

Vomiting, and negative reinforcement, 42